Picking Cotton in Corporate America

Survival Notes from The Invisible Plantation

Aubrey B. Jones, Jr.

PublishAmerica
Baltimore

© 2005 by Aubrey B. Jones, Jr.
All rights reserved. No part of this book may be reproduced, stored in a retrieval system or transmitted in any form or by any means without the prior written permission of the publishers, except by a reviewer who may quote brief passages in a review to be printed in a newspaper, magazine or journal.

First printing

At the specific preference of the author, PublishAmerica allowed this work to remain exactly as the author intended, verbatim, without editorial input.

ISBN: 1-4137-9368-1
PUBLISHED BY PUBLISHAMERICA, LLLP
www.publishamerica.com
Baltimore

Printed in the United States of America

This book is dedicated to:

My wife Diane

My Son, Aubrey III

My Daughter, Adrienne

"I am grateful to my teachers, co-workers, family and friends who helped shape my life because I learned something from each of you. I thank God for the privilege of writing this book and pray that this book will be a blessing to everyone who reads it."
Aubrey B. Jones, Jr.

Contents

Foreword 10
    A Black Man's Survival Notes 12
Preface 13
Introduction 19
Don't Get Stuck on the Plantation 19
    I'M A VSP 22
I. Growing up on the Richmond Plantation 25
    In the Beginning … 25
    Early Life on the Richmond Plantation 27
    The "White" Water Fountain 31
    School–A Respite from the Plantation 32
    I Can Do Better Than This! 34
        The Picture in My Mind 39
    The Black Church-A Place to be Somebody 40
        Free Gift! Unlimited Access! No Strings Attached! 43
II Escape to the U.S. Air Force's Plantation 46
    Where do I Go From Here? 46
        Choosing Your Career 48
    Wow! These Guys Aren't So Smart After All 50
        No Limits for Me! 52
    Biloxi Blues 53
    Deep in the Heart of Texas! 55
    Segregation Everywhere 58
    "Free at Last!" (Wonderful Copenhagen) 62
    Back Home to the Plantation 64
        A Goal 67
III Life on Mr. Jefferson's Plantation - UVA 68
    The Missing Application 68
    Six Things You Can Do To Get Ahead… 69
    I Can Do It Too! 70
    Behind the Scenes 75
    The Blacks are Coming! The Blacks are Coming! 77
    The No-Name Fraternity 80

Charter Members of UVA's No-Name Fraternity
(Undergraduate Chapter) 84
The Struggle Makes You Stronger 85
Blacks Who Attended UVA During Period 1950-1963* 87
Blacks Who Attended UVA During Period 1950-1963* 88
    Anger 90
The "Rat Pack" 92
Putting a Little Light on the Subject 93
    Words 96
I'm Out of Here 98
    You Can Do It Too! 100
The Interview 103
    GO FOR IT ! 105

IV. Life Philco-Ford's Plantation in the 1960s 106
How Does It Feel To Be Up North? 106
I Hate My Job 108
Showcase Blacks 110
(Excerpts of the letter to Mr. H.R. Mann) 112
Who Helped You Write That Letter 114
OEO Plant Visit 115
(Copy of Letter on OEO Visit) 116
Did it Do Any Good? 118
The Interview at IBM's Plantation 119
(Copy of the Letter to T. J. Watson, Jr) 120
Aftermath of the IBM Interview 123
(Copy of the Letter from T. J Watson, Jr.) 124
Gaining Respect on the Plantation 125
    Respect 128

V. The HNIC on Control Data's Plantation 129
My Transition from an Engineer to a Manager 129
My Unique Role at CDC 131
The Last Straw 135
(Copy of the letter to Mr. Norris) 136
Lessons Learned 141
    Thank You Very Much! 144

VI. The OREO HNIC - ISI 146
Life on a Small Corporate Plantation 146
Put a Little Bit Back into the Pot 147
Reflections on the Million Man March 151
Black is Beautiful 153
I'm An African-American 157
Back to the Fortune 500 Plantation 160
VII. Working On Sperry's Corporate Plantation 162
Do You Have a Chip on Your Shoulder? 162
Introduction to the Poem
"Pull Yourself Up by Your Roots!" 165
Pull Yourself Up By Your Roots! 166
Is It Because I'm Black? 168
(Letter to President Of Univac) 170
The Pen is Mightier than the Sword 173
You Receive Much More than You Give 177
Time to Move On 180
Ownership 185
VIII. Working on RCA Service Company's Plantation 186
It's a Dirty Job but a Slave has to Do It! 186
The Boss' Secretary 187
Work it Out!(Conflict Resolution) 190
Politics on the Plantation 193
A Female HNIC and the "Untouchables" 195
Downsized 199
(Letter to Chairman of GE.) 202
A Sobering Experience 205
Finding a Job on Another Plantation 206
IX. Life on an "Un-Managed" Plantation-DEC 210
A Rough Start 210
Skip a Level Meetings 213
Handling Prima Donnas 215
The "Matrix-Managed" Plantation 219
Leadership 224
The Blue Bell Plantation 225

"Black Notes"-The Communications Network 230
A Real HNIC 231
Valuing Diversity 235
Downsized Again 237
X. How to Get off the Plantation 243
Are You Ready to Leave the Plantation? 243
My Attitude–Controls My Altitude 245
There's Life After Downsizing 246
Stay in School 249
I'm Cool, I'm Bad, and I'm Almost Grown ... 252
Message to My Young Brothers and Sisters ... 254
If You Get Down Don't Stay Down! 256
I'm A Man but It's Okay To Cry 258
You're Not A Bum to Me! 260
Family Values 262
Family Matters 266
Kid's Rights 268
Black on Black Violence 269
Lessons I Learned From My First Wife 271
Finding The Perfect Mate 274
Lessons I Learned from My Current Wife 277
I'm A Winner! 279
Don't Become Too Complacent! 280
I'm The BO$$! 285
Success! 286
POWER 291
"All Things Work Together for Good ..." 292
Is That You God? 294
Epilogue: "I Can Do All Things Through Christ
   Who Strengthens Me!" 296
Final Quotations 300

List of Poems

A Black Man's Survival Notes	12
A Goal	67
Anger	90
Black on Black Violence	269
Choosing Your Career	48
Family Matters	266
Finding the Perfect Mate	274
Free Gift! Unlimited Access! No Strings Attached!	43
Go For It!	105
I'm An African American	157
I'm a Man But It's Okay to Cry	258
I'm A VSP	22
I'm A Winner!	279
I'm Cool, I'm Bad, and I'm Almost Grown	252
I'm The BO$$!	285
Is That You God?	294
Kids Rights	268
Leadership	224
Message to My Brothers and Sisters	254
My Attitude Controls My Altitude	245
No Limits For Me	52
Ownership	185
Picture In My Mind, The	39
Power	291
Pull Yourself Up By Your Roots	166
Reflections On the Million Man March	151
Respect	128
Thank You Very Much	144
Words	96
Work It Out! (Conflict Resolution)	190
You're not A Bum To Me!	260
You Can Do It Too!	100

Foreword

I first met Mr. Jones in the late 1950s, when he came to the University of Virginia after his Air Force service. I have been thrilled to meet with this truly remarkable man occasionally over the course of his career since his graduation. It is always a pleasure to hear about his good works and to share our memories of the times when he was a student at the University. My wife and I had lunch with him to discuss a book he had written about his experiences in industry, called *Picking Cotton in Corporate America*. I was honored to have been asked to read his manuscript.

This is an inspiring book, because it shows how a young Black man with determination, high intelligence, and deeply religious and humane instincts could "beat the system" over the course of the many years of struggle for civil rights. The book also includes his memories of his childhood days together with his military and higher education years. Mr. Jones is a model of how the worthy struggle can be fought by the individual against seemingly insuperable odds.

Reading the book, I felt I was listening to a real person, somebody who had "been there and done that." Aubrey has just enough details of his job experiences to make a convincing argument for his points, but not so much as to overwhelm the reader. It is the voice of a fighter, true, but not a super-hero who has set impossible goals for anyone else to follow. I wish I had

had him around when I was having tough career times of my own. I could have used some of his wisdom and his bravery! Another thing I like about the voice is that it conveys an acknowledgement that he had to work and spend quite some time to learn what he did. So, now he wants to tell others and, in effect, save them lots of time and struggle by telling them the paths to pursue that will likely yield some good results. The voice is upbeat and authoritative at the same time.

There are many things in the book that caught my attention, not the least of which were many pieces of practical advice—like the section on how to accept criticism. Or the excerpts from the letters that he wrote to the CEOs that show if you want action-start at the top. I know that if the readers are students or people, who work in the corporate world, read this section carefully, they'll get a lot out of it.

Finally, Aubrey includes poems and direct statements at the end of each chapter as to exactly what he learned (and hopes the readers will learn) from what went on in the chapter. This book is valuable beyond measure and everyone regardless of his or her age will enjoy reading it.

> Luther Y. Gore
> Emeritus Professor of Humanities
> School of Engineering and Applied Science
> University of Virginia

A Black Man's Survival Notes

By Aubrey B. Jones, Jr.

I wasn't a slave
But they tried to keep me on a plantation

I wasn't put in jail
But they tried to restrict my freedom

I wasn't beaten physically
But they tried to whip me mentally

I wasn't inferior
But they tried to brainwash me to believe it

I wasn't killed
But they tried to kill my spirit

I wasn't given any information
So I worked in the dark and showed them innovation

I wasn't allowed to have my religion
So God spoke to me through a vision

I wasn't suppose to survive
But I did

I was down, but never out
And that's what survival is all about!
"If it is to be, It's up to me
I can do it too!
"I can do all things through Christ Who strengthens me"
    (Philippians 4:13)

Preface

I want to pass it on! Pass on the lessons learned in my struggle for civil rights. Pass it on so that others can learn from and avoid making the same mistakes I made. Pass on how I "beat the system" designed to keep me down on the "invisible plantation."

I am old enough to have experienced segregation in the south but young enough to be one of the first Blacks to integrate the University of Virginia in 1958. I am old enough to remember the challenges for a Black man entering the U.S. Air Force in 1954 but young enough to be among the first Blacks to integrate Corporate America in 1963. With over thirty years experience working for five Fortune 500 corporations, I have seen a lot, heard a lot and done a lot. And with over twenty-five years of management experience, I truly have a different perspective of what really happens in the corporate world. The sad thing is that many of the things that happened some forty years ago are still happening today. Therefore, the information in this book is timeless and will be helpful for anyone who wants to read it.

When I started working in 1963, there were not many Blacks around in any capacity much less in management. Throughout this book, I point out some of the racial discrimination that went on over forty years ago and still goes on today. But just like forty years ago, many Whites deny or refuse to recognize that there are any problems. And even worse, our government is talking about doing away with affirmative action programs. People who want to get rid of affirmative action say that "discrimination" is a thing of the past and that such programs are no longer needed. They argue that at universities and corporations, there is now a "level playing field." But this is a lie. And the recent scandals at companies like Texaco provide a stark picture of the *systematic* institutional racism that exists in this country.

I wanted to write this book for some time but I just could never seem to get around to doing it. You never know why things happen in your life. Bored of my job, I knew that it was time for me to leave Digital Equipment Corporation. It was time to leave and use my talents elsewhere. In 1994, I was downsized from Digital and had all the time I needed to start writing a book. But it was not until my good friend, Carol Aycox, an English teacher, told me again, *"Tell Your Story!"* that I started to write. It was the spark that I needed to energize me. Carol had heard pieces of my story over the years and felt that it was a story to be shared with others. Another friend, Tom Garrett, suggested the title for the book some four years before I started to write it. He said to me one Sunday at church, "Aubrey! I have a great title for a book for you – **Picking Cotton in Corporate America!**" We both laughed and then I just forgot about it until I was looking for a working title for my book. That title led me to the metaphor of *life on a plantation* that provided the glue to hold my story together.

I started writing this book in 1994 but I did not complete my first draft until 1995. It is now 2005, and a lot of things happened in my life between 1995 and 2005. In 2004, my mother and my brother died. My mother's death was not a surprise because at 91 she had a full life. But my brother Ed's death, who was 13 months younger than I, was a shocker. When death comes to a person, like Ed, who had been terminally ill for several months, we are not prepared. In Ed's case, where death came relatively suddenly after seemingly being in good health, I found myself in a state of shock, as if I was in a dream world, unable to fully comprehend what had happened. He was my oldest, closest and dearest friend and we went through a lot of things together.

While he was in the hospital, perhaps the most significant thing happened a few months before he died. I visited him along with my daughter, Adrienne, and my son, Aubrey. He was in a good mood that day. After we were there for a few minutes, he said to me (jokingly) "I want you to leave the room because I have something to say." Then he said, *"I prayed last night for the first time, and a certain calmness and peacefulness came over me. I can't explain it. I believe in the Lord, there is no more doubt in my mind that he is real. – And I just didn't want to hear you say, I told you so!"*

You see Ed had been struggling with his belief for a while. Although he and I were baptized together at a very early age, he began to question certain things about the Bible. At one point, he told me that he wasn't sure what he believed because there were a lot of things he did not understand. So I was overjoyed when he told me that he knew the Lord, because I knew then, that he was going to be alright! I thank God for allowing Ed to be here for 68 years and I know he is going to be alright because he is together with the Lord. I love him and I miss him. Ed's death motivated me to finish this book because no one knows how much time we have left on this earth.

I have learned that life is full of obstacles and challenges and if you give up every time you are faced with a challenge, you will never accomplish anything. Let's face it, poverty, unemployment, AIDS, discrimination, politics and other challenges exist. But that should not stop you from achieving your goals. It did not stop Nelson Mandela from leading the fight against apartheid in South Africa while he was in prison. It did not stop Arthur Ashe from becoming a great tennis champion. It did not stop Martin Luther King from keeping a dream alive. And it must not stop you, me or anyone else from dreaming our dreams, setting our goals and making our dreams a reality.

It took me a while to really overcome the negatives in my life and to build up my self-esteem. I was brainwashed by the system designed to keep me down by trying to control my thoughts. But once I learned the secret of how to overcome all of the negativity, racism and other barriers, there was no stopping me from achieving my potential. I learned that it is ***not the circumstances that surround your life but how you respond to them is what makes the difference.***

I do not intend to embarrass any of my former coworkers or associates, and therefore, I have changed the names of those persons who were involved in controversial situations. Persons whose names were changed appear in *italics* in the book. Since I am "pack rat," I don't throw away anything. This trait came in very handy when trying to recall some things that happened over thirty years ago. I kept copies of the letters I wrote to the presidents of the major corporations. I kept copies of the responses to those letters and copies of interoffice memos that I wrote or received on various topics. These letters and memos together with an old manuscript for a book that I attempted to write in 1970 provided much of the background information used in this book. Of course, it was much easier for me to recall my experiences at RCA and Digital because they were my most recent jobs. For each company, I tried to highlight the most significant things that would be of interest to the reader.

My aim was to make this book short enough so someone could pick it up and read it in a short period of time. And it is my desire that the book will be used as a reference from time to time for those people who might need an emotional lift. Although it is suggested that you start with Chapter 1, you do not have to read each chapter in sequence to understand the messages in the book. It is possible to go to a specific chapter of interest to read and understand it without knowing all of the background. In short, I tried to make it more attractive for the casual reader who might just pick it up, scan the topics and then will be motivated to read it. I believe I have achieved my goal.

This book describes how I dealt with the challenges in my life and the valuable lessons I learned along the way. These lessons are shared in my stories and in the poems included in this book. I use poems which offer some thought provoking, practical suggestions on how to deal with some of the challenges in your life. A common theme in most of the poems emphasizes that if you have the *desire* and *belief,* you can overcome your obstacles. Each poem reinforces the various messages of the chapter. The messages in the book are timeless and are useful for people of all ages. After reading this book, I hope you will realize that **you have the power in you to be what you want to be** and with God's help you can do anything if you really **believe** that you can do it!

"It is not the circumstances that surround your life
But how you respond to them is what makes the difference."

Introduction

Don't Get Stuck on the Plantation

I have always been a fighter. The best way to get me fired up is to tell me that I can't do something especially when I feel it's the right thing to do. If you tell me that I'm not capable of doing something that I really want to do, watch me become ***energized*** to do whatever it takes to make it happen. I call it ***negative motivation*** and as a Black man growing up in the south, I needed to believe in myself despite all the negative things people around me said or did to discourage me. And as quiet as it is kept, all the negative things did not come from White folks. There were plenty of narrow-minded Black folks who for whatever reason tried to discourage me.

For, example, my high school electronics teacher told me that I would never be a good electronics technician. I really wanted to become a technician so I didn't listen to him. I went on to become a successful radio and radar maintenance technician in the Air Force. In 1955, when I visited my high school while on leave from the Air Force, my electronics teacher introduced me as one of his best students and how proud he was of my accomplishments in the Air Force. I never told him how I felt about his earlier comments to me because perhaps he thought he was helping me. This is only one of many times that I had to use my inner strength to succeed in spite of the negative influences around me.

A line from one of my poems, "I'm A VSP," best describes my fighting spirit. The poem says: *"Some people keep me in the dark and deny me information, so I've learned to work in the dark and show them innovation. I'm a VSP, A Very Special Person!"* I have learned when to pick my battles. Although I did not always win, I have always been able to look at myself in the mirror and feel good about myself because I knew that I had done my very best. But more importantly, I learned something with each of my challenges. I learned that the struggles made me stronger.

Some people who know me might be surprised to hear me say that I'm a fighter because I probably have given them the perception of being a laid back passive individual. But inside of me, there is the same rage that many Black men have because of their struggles for equality and manhood. The key to my success is that I learned to use the system. I learned the rules of the game and became very adept at playing the game. I learned a long time ago that an intelligent Black man intimidates the racists and bigots. The bigots know that if the brothers break the law that they can put them away for a long time. But a free thinking, intelligent Black man is seen as a threat. He works the system, understands the game, and is smart enough ***not*** to let them know that he has "peeped" their game. And, as a result, the outspoken intelligent Black man is looked upon as a threat by some people and becomes a marked man. If a Black man dares to challenge the power structure, there is a price to pay. He will probably be labeled as a troublemaker, plus he runs the risk of losing his job and many other things that he worked so hard to accomplish.

Don't get me wrong, I don't hate White people. I just don't trust many of them. I know that this is wrong. Christianity has taught me not to judge a person by the color of his or her skin. But I am still a work in process. I am trying to overcome the lessons learned from dealing with White people on the plantation. And to use an old cliché, "some of my best friends are White." When I talk to many of the brothers who work in the corporate environment, they recognize that they are slaves to the corporations. They **"pick the cotton"** or do whatever menial jobs are required to gain a share of the "good life." They know the rules for survival on this invisible plantation – "you don't *stand up to* your slave masters!" But if a Black man doesn't stand up when he is passed over for promotions or is treated unfairly on a consistent basis, he pays an even higher price. He loses self-respect and self-esteem. The challenge is to know when to pick your fights and then be prepared to deal with the consequences. Finally, If a Black man becomes too complacent and forgets from whence he came and refuses to speak up when he should, he will *become stuck on the invisible plantation Picking Cotton in Corporate America.*

"Some people might believe that I'm nobody
But I'm here to tell you I'm somebody."
"Some people keep me in the dark and deny me information
So I've learned to work in the dark and show them innovation
I'm a VSP – A Very Special Person!"

I'M A VSP
By Aubrey Jones, Jr.

I'm a VSP - A Very Special Person
I'm a VSP - A Very Special Person

Some people might believe that I'm nobody
But I'm here to tell you I am somebody
Some people might not like me because of the color of my skin
But I can rise above that I have the power within
Some people try to steer me in the wrong direction
But I have the power to make the right selection
Some people look for reasons to concede
But I look for ways of how to succeed

I'm a VSP - A Very Special Person
I'm a VSP - A Very Special Person

Some people say I can't do this or that
But I refuse to listen because I know where it's at
Some people would like me to settle for less
But I refuse to accept nothing but the best
Some people like to think that they're much smarter
So I take the challenge and work a little harder
Some keep me in the dark and deny me information

So I work in the dark and show them innovation

I'm a VSP - A Very Special Person
I'm a VSP - A Very Special Person

Here's the last thing I want to say
I hope you didn't misunderstand me today

This world is full of very special people
Because all men and women are created equal
I'm a very special person and believe it too
And there's another special person and that person is you
So what you do is to make it very clear
Repeat after me so everyone can hear

I'm a VSP - A Very Special Person
I'm a VSP - A Very Special Person

I. Growing up on the Richmond Plantation

In the Beginning ...

My struggle started on July 13, 1935. I was born fighting for my life because I am a surviving twin. My brother was stillborn but no one ever told me this until some 50 years later. When my brother, Ed, told me I was a twin, it hit me like a "ton of bricks." I did not believe him at first so I asked my mother if it was true. She said that she thought I knew this. I was dumbfounded because how could I have possible known this if no one ever told me. She had assumed my grandmother whom I was very close to had told me. Both she and my brother handled this piece of information as though it was no big deal. But it was a big deal to me! I don't know why but hearing that I had shared my mother's womb with a brother for nine months really upset me. Why was I spared? I talked with my pastor about my feelings and he said, "Perhaps you have to live for two people. God does not always reveal His full plan to us. We never know why things happen." Over the years, I have learned to accept God's will and get on with my life.

As the oldest of five brothers and sisters, I felt a responsibility at a very young age to take care of my siblings. I felt that I would somehow escape the poverty and would be able to provide a better life for my entire family. I had a vision, *a picture in my mind* of what I wanted to do. I did not know exactly how I would escape my situation but I knew that I would. As I got older, this picture became clearer to me. Over the years, I have learned some important things about life and how you should live it. As a father, I accepted the responsibility to be there for my kids. I learned that if I had a choice between a business opportunity and my family, *my family came first*.

Earlier in life, I took the conservative or safe route because I did not ever want to be poor again. I did not want to subject my family to the same conditions I had to grow up under. I felt that if I failed there was no safety net for me or no one to bail me out. So I took limited risks which possibly limited my advancement somewhat. But, if I had to do it all over again, I would take the same path. Family and peace of mind were more important to me than trying to make a lot of money. It was more important that I survive as a whole person with a well-balanced life. As a Black man, I have accepted the responsibility to be a role model. We need more Black male role models to counter the negative perceptions many people have about Black men in general. I recognize the need to and mentor young people on survival skills for the world today. We need to *show* them *how to do it* and not just *tell them* how they should do it. We need to *lead by example!*

"I have a picture in my mind of what I really want to do
I will hold that picture in my mind until my dream comes true
I have a picture in my mind of what I really want to be
And nobody is going to steal that picture from me."

Early Life on the Richmond Plantation

My father was 47 years old and my mother was 22 when I was born. I do not remember too many things about the early part of my life. I can only imagine how rough it was for my parents who were Black, poor and living in the south a few years after the great depression of 1929. I knew my mother was born "out of wedlock" and was raised by foster parents, Mr. and Mrs. Goodwin. Although my mother knew her real mother, there was never any attempt to develop a relationship. According to my mother, her real father was a prominent Black doctor who looked like a white man. I have a picture that he had given to her years ago and on the back it was written "To My daughter." My mother never had much contact with her father. She also has a half brother that people say I resemble. Although he knew we were related, he never admitted it to me even though I saw him on numerous occasions. People did not talk openly about out of wedlock births. It was a stigma to have a child out of wedlock. So what was done sometimes, as in my mother's case, a private arrangement was made to give the child to a childless couple. As far as I was concerned Kate Goodwin, who we called "Big Ma," was my grandmother and Barton Goodwin was my grandfather on my mother's side.

I did not know a lot about my father's family either. I knew grandma Fannie Jones but her husband, Stephen Napoleon Bonapart Jones, died before I was born. I had assumed that my family's roots were in Richmond. But I learned many years later that my great grandfather on my father's side came from Charleston, South Carolina. This information was in the front of an old Bible. My great grandfather was a former African Chief who escaped from the Port of Charleston, South Carolina with some Indians (I don't know the tribe). He came to Richmond in 1864 and worked as a cook. My grandfather, Stephen, was the only child who survived to adulthood. My father was the youngest of three children and the last survivor. He died on August 28, 1982 at the age of 96 years. He was the last of the "old line" Jones' family which had been in Richmond for over 125 years.

I grew up in the Navy Hill section of Richmond. We lived at 608 north Eighth Street until I graduated from high school. Navy Hill Elementary School was a few blocks away and the city dump was down the street from me. Living up the street from the dump was not very pleasant, especially when the wind was blowing the wrong way, not to mention the rats, bugs and other things it attracted. It was not unusual to see big rats in your back yard or even in your house. We were fortunate that no one in my family was ever bitten by a rat. Everyone used rat traps or poison to try to control the rat infestation. At night, you could hear the rats moving inside the crumbling plaster walls. Before entering a room after dark, we would stomp on the floor loudly to announce our coming to the rats. This allowed them time to scurry back into their holes in the wall.

The city dump had some benefits too if you were a scavenger. We would search through piles of trash looking for items of value. Most homes in my neighborhood had no central heating system. No hot water to take a bath unless you heated it on the stove first. No thermostat to set the temperature or to turn up the heat when it got cold. We had to chop wood for kindling so that we could start a fire in the stove to heat the room. If the fire went out during the night, the house was cold when you woke up in the morning. So my brother, Ed, and I would take turns making a fire in the morning. After we made the fire, we would jump back under the covers until the room was warm enough for us to get up. Fortunately, the winters in Richmond were not severe but they were cold enough for me. After I was married, two things I always made certain we had in my house: plenty of food and plenty of heat. I never wanted to be cold or hungry again in life.

Some years later the city dump closed. They plowed it over, laid down some black top and transformed the city dump into the Navy Hill playground. This was great for the neighborhood because we had a place to play. There were sliding boards, swings and sandboxes. We had a baseball diamond where both little league and adults played their games. We had basketball courts and a field where we played football. It was also a community gathering place, especially during the summer, because there were lights for evening activities. After the playground closed for the evening, we would spend the long summer evenings on the porch until the bedrooms cooled enough to allow sleep. No one locked doors or windows in the neighborhood. Our neighborhood was relatively safe. Everybody knew and spoke to their neighbors. Occasionally, on Friday and Saturday evenings, there would be fights at the bar at the corner. Technically, it was not a bar because Virginia's laws did not permit the sale of wine or whiskey by the drink. You could only buy beer. There were no gang wars, no drive by shootings and no drugs. In short, we were a poor hard working Black community trying to make it in a society that was geared to keep us down on the plantation.

I was six years old in 1941. I remember World War II because there were soldiers stationed in an armory down the street from my house in Richmond. What I remember most of all were the army trucks, jeeps, weapons and the candy. During the war, everything was rationed including gasoline, nylons and candy. Soldiers could get as much candy as they wanted and they would always give candy to the neighborhood kids. Then there were the frequent blackouts and the mock air raids. For those of you too young to remember, many cities prepared for air raids by having drills much like fire drills today. During an air raid drill, everyone had to turn off the lights in their homes when the sirens sounded. The cities were blacked out so that a low flying plane could not find targets. There was no sophisticated radar, infrared, or missile systems to locate targets at night. Some people were designated in our neighborhood as air raid wardens who walked along the streets to make sure all lights were out. They wore white helmets and carried flashlights as they patrolled the streets looking for violators. If your lights were on, you had to use blackout shades at you windows so that light would not shine through the windows. At school, we would have air raid drills where everyone would go to the basement or into the hallways of the school. Throughout the city were designated areas for air raid shelters where you could go to if you were not at home.

We had a great national spirit in our country then because we were fighting a common enemy. Although Blacks were treated as second class citizens, we were proud to be Americans and were willing to die for our country. Many young Black men died during WWII so that we could enjoy freedom and have all the rights and privileges of being a citizen of this country. Unfortunately, when the Black soldiers returned home from the war, they found out that ***nothing had changed on the plantation***. Today, we have come a long way but we are still not there yet for Blacks and other minorities.

"It not important where you start
But how you finish is what counts"

The "White" Water Fountain

Everyone in my neighborhood was poor. Some poorer than others but as a kid I did not realize that I was poor because everyone around me was poor. As a Black kid growing up in the south, I lived in an all Black community, attended an all Black church; went to segregated schools and movies. I was not really aware of segregation until I went downtown. We were sheltered as kids from many of the ills of segregation by our parents and our community. When I was very young, I remember going downtown with my grandmother. While we were in W.T. Grants department store, I was thirsty so I went to drink out of the water fountain and my grandmother pulled me away. So I asked her, "Why can't I drink out of that water fountain?" She said, "That's for White folks son." Although I did not fully understand why I could not drink out of the *White* water fountain, I remember saying to myself, "What's so special about the *White* water fountain?" That was the first time I remember encountering segregation but it was not my last.

One day when I was much older, I went downtown by myself and stopped by W.T. Grants. I walked over to the *"White water fountain,"* looked around to see if anyone was watching me and then I sneaked a drink from the *"White"* water fountain. I ran like hell out of the door into the street as though I had done something wrong. "Yes," I got me a drink out of the *"White water fountain"* and nobody was going to stop me now! Nobody did from then on, because I was one of the more fortunate Blacks who escaped from a system designed to keep me down. A system that skillfully brainwashed me to accept the White man's theory that I was inferior because I was born Black. A system that forced me to use separate toilets, to stand or sit at segregated lunch counters and to ride on the back of the bus. A system that made me feel like a second or third class citizen. There used to be a saying *"If you're white you're all right, if you're brown you can stick around, but if you are black, stand back!"* I used to laugh when I heard this saying because I didn't know any better. I didn't realize then that I was being brainwashed while *living on this invisible plantation.*

"*I wasn't beaten physically
But they tried to whip me mentally
I wasn't inferior
But they tried to brainwash me to believe it.
I was down but never out
That's what survival is all about.*"

School–A Respite from the Plantation

School was always very important to me. It was a special place for me where I could escape the reality of where I lived and how I lived. It was a place staffed with dedicated teachers who really cared about us. I could live in a fantasy, I could dream, I could escape. In school, we *learned* despite having inadequate facilities. We *learned* despite using old ragged hand me down books discarded by the white schools because we had the will to learn instilled in us by teachers who really cared about us. Teachers had the support of the parents and the respect of the students because most parents believed that the teachers had their children's best interest in mind. As a result, I was motivated to learn and I thank all of my teachers for their dedication and support.

Two of my eighth grade teachers taught me some things that I have always remembered and these things helped build my character. One teacher, Mrs. Seagar, made us recite a poem entitled *"Be the Best of Whatever You Are!"* Although I did not fully appreciate the poem then, it set the standard for me to always strive to be the best. As the poem suggested, it did not matter what you attempted to do, just be the best and be proud of what you have done. Mr. Fred Lewis was a brilliant math teacher who fascinated me with his quick wit and knowledge of math. He always had a quote for most situations. Two of my favorites are: 1) *"There are no shortcuts and to he who has patience the end will be well worth the journey"* and 2) *"A person who is good at making excuses is seldom good at anything else."* Most people who know me have heard me use these quotes often. I am sure my kids have grown tired of hearing me use these quotes around them.

I really enjoyed high school. One of the activities that I enjoyed most was the Cadet Corps. All of the high schools in Richmond had Cadet Corps, which were like a junior ROTC. We learned discipline and we participated in parades for both school and civic events. Oftentimes, we would participate in a city parade. One of the biggest parades was the Tobacco Festival, which was an annual event in Richmond. It was a very colorful event with lots of floats bands and marchers. They would always put Blacks at the end of the parade. One year, we refused to march because they put us at the end of the parade. It made the news because that was the first time, as I recall, that Blacks had ever protested about being last in line. I was both disappointed and happy about the decision. I enjoyed marching but I understood that sometimes you have to make a personal sacrifice for a greater good. This was my first but not the last time that I was able to be a part of something that ultimately would make a difference.

There were two Black high schools in Richmond, Armstrong and Maggie L. Walker. I attended Armstrong, a bitter rival of Walker, especially in football. Every year on the Saturday after

Thanksgiving, there was "The Game"-Amstrong vs. Walker. This game was so big it had to be held at the city stadium. A crowd of 20,000 to 30,000 would attend this high school classic. Alumni would return for this game. In fact, I attended almost every game after I graduated from high school except for the period of time that I was in the Air Force. People really dressed up for this game. It was a fashion show. It was a homecoming. It was "a happening" in Richmond. The last game was played in 1978 because Armstrong and Maggie L. Walker no longer existed as an entity after that year. That is, each of these schools was merged with other schools. A price we had to pay because of integration. I was at that last game, and it was a sad day for Blacks in Richmond. We were never able to capture that spirit again although we tried by substituting other games in its place. But thanks for the memories.

"Be The Best of Whatever You Are!"

"There are no shortcuts and to he who has patience the end will be well worth the journey."

"A person who is good at making excuses is seldom good at anything else."

I Can Do Better Than This!

I was the first person in my immediate family to graduate from high school. My father went to the third grade. He was a self-taught and a very articulate man for the amount of formal education he had received. He learned by reading books on ready made speeches. He even had a book on "Roberts Rules of Order" which prepared him to hold office in the Elks. His passion was the ELKS. He spent many of his hours at the William's Lodge Elks Home in Richmond. I remember him referring to some people as "educated fools." They were people who had book smarts and degrees but no common sense. He told me, *"The mark of an educated man is someone who can talk to people at all levels."* Later in life I realized what he was trying to tell me. That is, you should not have to be a PHD to understand a PHD. You should be able to make a presentation in the boardroom of a corporation, and still be able to talk to the brothers on the corner if you wanted to do so. Perhaps that planted the seed for one of my strengths, "being able to simplify complex information so that the average person can understand it."

Selling whiskey by the drink was illegal in Virginia during the 1950s. The only way to get around that law legally was to join a private club or association. As a member of the ELKS club, you could keep alcoholic beverages in your locker and you could serve drinks to your guests. There were also illegal ways of selling alcoholic drinks by becoming a bootlegger. We had three or four in my neighborhood. Occasionally the police raided them but oftentimes you would see the police stop by and it was rumored that the cops received payoffs to let the bootlegger operate.

I believe my mother went to the tenth grade. She worked primarily as a waitress. My mother was fair skinned so she could get jobs in some places where other Blacks could not. Although it was obvious that my mother was Black, there were times when Blacks passed for white so that they could get a higher paying job or just get a job. My father worked in the U.S. Post

Office as an elevator operator, which paid pretty good relatively speaking. He often threatened to make me quit school and get a job. He said I did not need a high school education to get a job because he had a "good job" and he only completed the third grade.

My dream was to finish high school. I knew that I could not do a lot with just a high school diploma but my prospects of a career without a diploma were even worse. As a result, I got an after school job selling papers. I was a hustler. I started out selling 25 papers a day until I moved up to a location that sold 250 papers a day. To put this into proper perspective, 250 papers at a profit of 2 cents per copy earned me $5.00 per day or $30.00 per week. During the summer, I sold morning papers also, and this increased my earnings to $60.00 per week, which was twice as much as many adults were making on full time jobs. On Saturday mornings, my brother, Ed, and I shined shoes and earned another $5.00 to $10.00. Part of my earnings went to my mother to help with the household expenses.

My maternal grandmother, Kate Goodwin, taught me about saving money and showed me how to open up a savings account in a bank. I learned to save part of whatever you earned. I also learned that it is not necessarily how much you make but what you do with what you make. My grandmother was a domestic worker and my grandfather was a laborer. But they were able to buy a house, own a car and still save some money. On the other hand, my father who was an honest, hard-working man was always in debt. He never owned a car or a home and he never opened up a bank account. There were a number of reasons my father could never get ahead. One reason was that he bought all of our food *"on the book."* Buying *on the book* was a common practice in my neighborhood. There was a Jewish owned grocery store in the neighborhood that would let some of the customers by food on credit but at very inflated prices. When you went to the store to buy something, the storeowner would add up the total for your purchases and enter this amount under your account in his general ledger. The owner in turn would enter the same amount in your little book for your record (That's where the expression *"buying on the book"* came from). A major problem with buying on the book is that the owner put whatever he wanted to in the book. I recall one time of adding up the total in my head and I came up with a different total than the owner and I challenged him. He checked his numbers and then patted me on my head and said, "you're a smart little boy!" I wondered how many times he overcharged my father and others.

My father got paid once a month. After he paid the rent, the food bill and other debts, he did not have any money left. Therefore, in order for us to eat, he had to continue to buy on the book. He was *"hooked on the book."* In addition to buying on the book, my father got further into debt using the so-called easy credit terms of the many stores that sold furniture, clothes and anything else you needed. Again the credit was easy because of the inflated prices and the high interest rates that were charged by these stores. You would see the easy credit terms signs all over the city, which sucked in the unsuspecting Blacks to get deeper in debt. Then there were the loan companies where you could borrow from $50.00 to $500.00 with no collateral but you paid the price in the interest rates. Loan companies did a thriving business because most banks would not loan money to Black people even to buy a house.

After seeing my father struggle to pay his bills, I vowed that I would not live like that when I became a man. Seeing my father struggle just made me work harder at hustling my papers and studying for school so that I could graduate from high school. I didn't know what would happen after high school but I knew I had to graduate first. With a high school diploma, I could not do a lot, but without one I could do even less. I knew that I had to escape this poverty and make a better life for myself. I was determined that I could and would provide a better life for my family. I was determined to escape the invisible plantation.

"Surviving and living your life successfully requires courage.

The goals and dreams you're seeking require courage and risk taking."

The Picture in My Mind
by Aubrey B. Jones Jr.

I have a picture in my mind of what I really want to do.
I will hold this picture in my mind until my dream comes true.
I have a picture in my mind of what I really want to be.
And nobody is going to steal this picture from me.

There is a picture in my mind of what I want to be
I will *focus* on this picture because *it really looks good* to me.
I see myself doing some things that I thought *impossible* to do
But a little *voice* inside keeps telling me that *"I Can Do It Too!"*
Now that I have this picture where do I go from here?
I will just hold that picture in my mind and keep it very clear.

I have a picture in my mind of what I really want to do.
I will hold this picture in my mind until my dream comes true.
I have a picture in my mind of what I really want to be.
And nobody is going to steal this picture from me.

Hold that picture in your mind and don't let anyone steal it from you!
Don't let your *present situation* keep your *dream* from coming true.
Think about the things that you need to do.
Because a picture *alone* won't make it happen for you!
You must *write down your goals* and keep them in view.

Then **Work** and **Work** and **Work** until your
dream comes true.

The Black Church-A Place to be Somebody

I can't talk about life in the south without mentioning the church. Most Blacks went to church on a regular basis or at least occasionally. Preachers were respected in the community because they had a captive audience every Sunday morning. We had to go to Sunday school and church every Sunday. My father made us go to church and one of the incentives to go to church was the movies. You see, if we did not attend church, we could not go to the movies on Sunday. And before TV was prevalent, going to the movies was a favorite pastime for almost everyone. I believe that Blacks were much more spiritual when I grew up then we are today. And because of our strong faith and belief in God, we were able to deal with segregation and all of the demeaning things that we faced each day. It is no surprise why during the sixties Black leadership came from the church. The church was the center of the power structure in the Black community. It was a big deal to be a deacon or a trustee at a Baptist church. That is, you could be a janitor in a department store during the week but on Sunday, you were Deacon Jones or Mr. Smith, Chairman of the Trustees.

Sunday was the one time everyone dressed up. Most folks always managed to get new outfits for Easter and Christmas but especially on Easter Sunday where everyone showed off his or her finest. Church was also a place for young people to meet and socialize. Although I did not consider myself a devout Christian, I believed in God and I know now that if it were not for Him I would not have made this far. But like many other young people, I stopped attending church on a regular basis when I was 18 years old. It appears that many young people drop out of attending church between the ages of 18 to 25 years. Many of us did not attend church because we were attending college or in the military and used the excuse that we could not find any "good churches" to attend. I realize now that these were poor excuses and that I was just exercising a new freedom of choice that I had attained. For the most part, I did not start attending church on a regular basis until 1975.

In 1975, I was invited to visit Salem Baptist Church in Jenkintown, Pennsylvania. It was Layperson's Sunday and they had a guest speaker, Congressman Harold Ford from Tennessee. In his sermon, he told the congregation to make time for God. He said that we made time for everything else that we wanted to do but we always found an excuse when it came to serving God. Well he certainly stepped on a lot of toes that Sunday including mine. For someone who was forced to go to church as a kid, I just seemed to drift away from it as I got older. So I decided to do something I should have done long before then, and that was to join a church.

Salem came into my life at the right time. It really helped me to focus on the right priorities. I realized that everything that I had, I owed it to God and the least that I could do was to thank Him for it by going to church and praising Him. I really got caught up in the church. There was nothing they would ask me to do that I would not do except sing on the choir. Singing was not one of my God given talents. My life turned around after joining Salem and I gained an extended supportive family. I attended church and Sunday school every Sunday because it was like a spiritual gas station for me. I needed to get a "fill-up" on Sunday so I could deal with the challenges of the next week. When I faced major challenges in my life, I had a little prayer that I would repeat and it gave me the strength I needed. It helped me face problems on and off the job. This prayer affirmed my belief that all things are possible through God. My prayer was: *"Lord, help me to remember that nothing is going to happen today that you and I together can't handle."*

We need to get back to our strong faith and belief in God and to remember that all things are possible through Him. Some Blacks have forgotten about the struggles of the past and believe that they have made it on their own. But the struggle is never over. Even if you are a slave on a plantation, you are always somebody in the eyes of God. When you are active in your church, you have a chance to get away from the plantation. You have the chance to feel good about yourself and realize that you are somebody-A very special person in the eyes of your community and God.

"I can do all things through Christ who strengthens me."
(Philippians 4:13)

Free Gift! Unlimited Access! No Strings Attached!

By Aubrey B. Jones, Jr.

> Free! Unlimited (24x7) Access!
> No Strings Attached!
> Yes! Completely Free!
> No Hidden Costs!
> Accept this Offer Today!
> Time is Running Out!

Advertisers know that one of the words that attract people is the word "Free."
They know that people are always looking for something for nothing.
Some people respond even if they suspect that there are some strings attached.
They respond even if they suspect that there are some hidden costs in the contract.
There is something magical about the word "free" that makes you to want to check it out.
There is something compelling about this word that makes you to want to take a chance.
Yet there is a free gift available to everyone that many people won't even talk about
So why do so many people pass on this gift without even checking it out?

Suppose someone told you that there was a free gift waiting for you.
Suppose you were told that it was a *life-changing gift,* what would you do?
You could accept it or reject it - if you don't believe it's true.
You can accept it, reject it or ignore it! - It's all up to you.
Let me assure you that this *free life-changing gift* is available today.
It is an unconditional gift with no hidden costs or fees to pay.
So what is this *life-changing gift* that you are talking about?
How do I receive this gift because I still have some doubt?
Well, I am talking about the gift of salvation.
You can receive this gift if you just follow this biblical quotation:

> "Confess with your mouth that Jesus is Lord
> And believe in your heart that God raised Him from the dead, and you will be saved.
> For it is by believing in your heart that you are made right with God,
> And it is by confessing with your mouth that you are saved."

You mean to tell me it's that simple to do?
Yes, salvation is as close as your own lips and your heart, but it's really up to you.

If you believe in your heart and say it with your mouth that Christ is the risen Lord, then you will be saved.
If you believe in your heart and want to be saved, He will come to you wherever you are.
No strings attached, no hidden costs, all you need to do is to respond and accept His gift.
No strings attached it's completely free, but you must accept it on your own free will.
It's a gift from God with unlimited access to Him 24 hours a day.
Believe this in your heart, confess your sins and *accept this free gift today!*

>Free! Unlimited (24x7) Access!
>No Strings Attached!
>Yes! Completely Free!
>No Hidden Costs!
>Accept This Offer Today!
>Time is Running Out!

II Escape to the U.S. Air Force's Plantation

Where do I Go From Here?

After I graduated from high school, I did not know what I was going to do. I did not have any money to go to college. Nor did I know what I would take even if I could have afforded to go to college. In the eighth grade, we were supposed to select a career that we thought we might want to pursue. I thought that I might be interested in becoming a lawyer. As part of a school's project, I had the opportunity to interview one of Richmond's finest Black Attorneys, Spottswood Robinson. My second choice was to become a railway mail clerk and my third choice was to become a mailman. When I was making these choices, it was in 1949 and there were not a lot of professional opportunities for Blacks.

To be considered successful in the eyes of the Black community in Richmond, you could pick one of "The Big 5." These were "Doctor, Lawyer, Teacher, Preacher or work in the U.S. Post Office." So I decided to select law although I knew that I really didn't want to be a lawyer but I had to pick something. I do not believe that we had any Black engineers in Richmond then. I never thought about engineering as a career until after I joined the Air Force. Maybe our teachers and counselors never told us about careers that were not open to Blacks so that we would not set unrealistic goals. Or maybe they were not aware of some of these careers themselves. The good news was that because I picked law as my career goal, I was able to take college preparatory courses instead of general studies courses.

Something happened along the way that changed my career goal. I took a course in basic electricity in high school during my senior year and really enjoyed it. I learned how to repair radios and televisions. So I decided that I wanted be a radio repairman because that was all I had been exposed to at that time. Even after graduation, I returned to high school as a post-graduate to take an advance course in electronics. I worked for a year as a stock clerk in Thalhimers department store making much less money than when I was selling papers. I was too embarrassed to be seen working as a stock clerk while many of my high school classmates were attending college. Therefore, I decided to join the Air Force so that I could attend electronics school and be eligible for the GI Bill that would pay for my college education. But more importantly, I thought that I could escape the invisible plantation.

Choosing Your Career

By Aubrey B. Jones, Jr.

I have the power in me to choose what I want to be
I have the power in me to choose what I want to be

Listen everybody and you shall hear about what to do when choosing your career
If you want to get a start on your career today then you better listen to what I'm about to say
You can be anything that you want to be If you say to yourself it's up to me
So let's listen - to see how to start; So let's listen - to see how to start.

Now here's the first thing that you should do; list those things that are important to you
If you say to yourself "I just don't know because I'm still undecided on which way to go?"
Then think about things that sound exciting to do; don't let your present situation be an obstacle to you
So let's think - and dream your dreams! so let's think - and dream your dreams!

When you finish high school you might find that joining the service will help you make up your mind
"Joining the service?" you might ask in a loud voice that's certainly not my first choice!
Well, you could get a job that pays minimum wage but how much will you be making when you reach middle age?
Think big - don't settle for less; think big - don't settle for less!

A Doctor, Lawyer, Teacher or Engineer? Boy, what an exciting career!

Programming, Accounting, and Marketing too? Could any of these be the right fit for you?

Professional or Corporate or Self-Employed? You pick the one that will be the most enjoyed

You make that choice - I know you can. You make that choice - I know you can.

If you want to go to college but you don't know what to do, then ask some questions about the college near you

If you feel that college is not the right direction; maybe a tech or trade school is your best selection

If you are still undecided about what you should do; then keep on searching until you find the right clue

So get busy - don't waste your time! So get busy - don't waste your time!

Here's the last thing that I want to say; I hope that you've learned something today

It does not matter what you want to be as long as you are the best that you can be

So when you decide on what you want to do just go for it! And good luck to you!

> *I have the power in me to choose what I want to be*
> *I have the power in me to choose what I want to be*

Wow! These Guys Aren't So Smart After All

On March 3, 1954, I enlisted in the U.S. Air Force. It was more difficult for a Black man to join the Air Force than the army because the Air Force was more selective on whom they would let enlist. For many of the Air Force job codes, you were taught a skill. My primary interest was to attend Electronics School and become a radio maintenance man. Before you were assigned a job code or AFSC (Air Force Specialty Code) you were tested. I scored highest on electronics and mechanics. But they told you up front that there were no guarantees because *"the needs of the Air Force came first."* Translated, it meant if they needed you as a cook, you became a cook. But I was fortunate because I got my first choice, "Electronics." Interestingly, I was assigned to radar school after electronics instead of radio. I was a little disappointed because I did not know anything about radar. Actually it was the better of the two schools although I did not know this at that time.

I was a member of Flight 3182, which had a mixture of airman from the north and the south. Most of the airman in my flight came from Virginia, the Carolinas, Pennsylvania, New York, Massachusetts and West Virginia. The White airman verbally fought the civil war over and over every day. There were approximately sixty-five men in my flight of which twelve were Black. One of my homeboys, Stuart Anderson, was also in my flight. When you are in the service, you bond with people from your state and especially with someone from the same town. One thing bothered me while I was in Basic training. Occasionally, some of the White airman from the north would call me a rebel or "Johnny Reb" because I was from the south. I was really annoyed with them for calling me a rebel. But they kept doing it until one day I said, "Have you guys ever seen a *colored rebel*? I don't like being called a rebel because it is demeaning to me" (Actually, I used much stronger language.). They stopped calling me a rebel after that.

Basic Training was not bad except for the weather. It was very cold especially when that wind whipped in off the lakes. I was stationed at Sampson Air Force Base in Geneva New York located right on the Finger Lakes. Many of the airmen complained about the food but I was eating much better there than I was eating at home. Because I was in the cadet corps at Armstrong High School, basic training was a snap for me. Discipline was not a problem because I knew how to march, call cadence and do the manual of arms with my weapon. My cadet corps experience worked in my favor because I was selected as a squad leader, which meant I got to wear the so-called "candy stripes" during basic training. In addition to the stripes, I received some perks, one of them being I did not have to do KP (Kitchen Police).

Joining the Air Force opened my eyes and helped destroy some of the myths that I had grown up believing that were true. It was my first experience living in an integrated environment and this experience helped improve my self-esteem. The Air Force helped destroy the myth that all White folks were smarter than Blacks. It helped me see the possibilities and exposed me to people and places that impacted my life. I remember how elated I was to learn that I had received the second highest score in an electronics course where I was the only Black in that class. I said to myself *"Wow! These guys aren't so smart after all."* It was a real shot in the arm for me, a real confidence building experience. It was the best anti-brainwashing treatment, the best medicine to straighten out my head. It transformed me from a person with low self-esteem to a person whose eyes were opened to the unlimited possibilities that awaited me. *I could really dream now!* Without question, joining the Air Force was one of the best decisions I have ever made. My tour of duty in the Air Force helped broaden my horizon. I was able to escape the segregated environment that was meant to keep me down. I was able to escape from the plantation in Richmond.

No Limits for Me!
Aubrey B. Jones, Jr.

I'm a person who can soar very high
I'm a person who can reach the sky
I could be a doctor, lawyer, teacher or engineer
Or I can choose some other exciting career
I'm a person who can choose what I want to be
I'm a person who has *no limits* set for me

> I can soar very high
> I can reach the sky
> I can choose what I want to be
> There *are no limits* set for me!

I'm a person who can soar above and beyond
I'm a person who knows how to respond
When something seems like an impossible situation
I approach it with a lot of faith and determination
I think **Big** and I don't settle for less
I'm a person who expects nothing but the **Best!**

> I can soar very high
> I can reach the sky
> I can choose what I want to be
> There *are no limits* set for me!

Biloxi Blues

After Basic Training, I was shipped to Keesler Air Force Base in Biloxi, Mississippi. Compared to Sampson Air force Base, this was paradise. All we had to do for five days a week was to go to school to learn electronics. The Air Force had the best electronics training program of all the services. They had the ability to take a civilian with no experience and teach him electronics in six months. This was a very intensive training course that would have probably taken me two years to complete in college or a trade school. Of course there were occasional inspections and KP but nothing like Basic Training. We had a lot more freedom at Keesler. There was everything you needed on the base except women. There were three movies with first run movies, swimming pools, Airmen's Club and other facilities.

One thing you had to remember was that you were in Mississippi and when you left the base, which was federal government property, you had to abide by the local segregation laws. For example, Keesler was larger than the town of Biloxi. The city bus ran its route through the base. As long as the bus was on the base, Blacks could sit anywhere they wanted to on the bus. But as soon as the bus went through the gates to the city we had to move to the back of the bus. Black and White airmen could share taxis to and from town but they could not hang out together while in town. Although I grew up in Richmond, Biloxi was hard for me to take so I stayed away from town. Instead, I would catch a bus on weekends and go to New Orleans.

New Orleans was a segregated city also but it was much larger than Biloxi and had a much larger Black population. Another benefit of going to New Orleans was that I could visit Xavier University where two of my high school classmates played football. Having my homeboys at Xavier made it easier for me to get introduced to some of the most attractive women

I had ever seen. At Xavier, I thought I had died and gone to heaven because I had not seen so my beautiful Black women in one place in my life. I loved New Orleans and went there every time I had the opportunity. Sometimes during the day, I would just stand at the corner of Rampart and Canal streets (a major intersection) and just enjoy the sights. In 1955, I had the chance to go to New Orleans for a Mardi Gras and it was one wild city during that time.

Several things happened at Keesler that were constant reminders that we were still in the segregated south. Many of the Blacks from up north had a very difficult time in Mississippi. I remember when all of the Black airmen were ordered to come to the chapel for a meeting with a Black chaplain. No one told us what the meeting was about beforehand but we were ordered to go. All of the Black airman had to get into a formation and march to the chapel. It was quite an unusual sight to see a large group of Black airman marching together. White airmen probably thought we were making some kind of orderly protest march because it was uncommon to see a group of Blacks marching together. All formations in the air force were usually integrated with more whites than blacks. When we got to the chapel, the chaplain read a list of ordinances which specified the things we could or could not do in town. He stressed that we had to abide by the local laws. That message did not go over too well with some of the brothers and many put in for transfers to another base. But my mission was to get an education and if it meant that I had to stay on the base until I completed my curriculum, then so be it.

Another thing I remember was that we had airmen from the Korean Air Force in some of our classes. These were very dedicated people who had one purpose only and that was to complete the course with the highest grade possible. Since they recognized that I was one of the better students in the class they asked if they could study with me sometimes. Most of them understood English although they did not speak it very well. Nevertheless, we studied together. But the most interesting thing was that after we finished studying together, they went back to their barracks and studied some more. Their grades reflected their effort because they were always near the top of the class. Their work ethics influenced me. If they could *not* speak the language as well as I could and were getting good grades then I realized that I should have an advantage over them if I studied a little harder too.

Although the Air Force was supposed to be completely integrated, they kept track of how many Blacks received promotions and other things. After an airman graduated from six months of Basic Electronics, he received another stripe automatically. The promotions were posted on the bulletin board. Someone noticed that there was an "N" beside my name within parenthesis. He asked me why the "N" was beside my name. At first, I said, "I don't Know" because I really did not know. Then I looked for the names of other Blacks and noticed that they also had an "N" beside their names so I realized that the "N" stood for Negro. The Air Force was keeping track of how many Blacks were being promoted. No matter how much I tried to feel like I was one of the guys, there were still little reminders to say that the system thinks that I am different. Again, I realized that *I was still on a plantation but at a different location and with a different slave master.*

Deep in the Heart of Texas!

When I completed my training at Keesler, I was assigned to Ellington Air Force Base near Houston, Texas. Ellington in 1956 trained navigators. My job was to provide maintenance on the navigational aid equipment that was installed in the flying classrooms. Each plane had 10 to 12 positions that were set up for the students to learn and practice their navigational skills. The first thing an old sergeant told us was to "forget everything we had learned in school." He reminded us that *"there was the right way, the wrong way and the air force way of doing things."* He was right because the theory helps you to understand "why," but you better know "how," if you want to be a good maintenance man. I was fascinated with my job because I had to work on planes parked on the flight line. Although I had studied and practiced on the radar equipment, it looked different to me installed in the plane.

The summer in Houston was hot and we slept in barracks that had no air conditioning. On the flight line, however, the radio shack (as it was called), where we waited for our next assignments, was air-conditioned. But much of our time was spent on the hot flight line working on equipment in the planes. I remember having to go into the tail section of the plane, which was a sealed compartment, to remove and replace a piece of equipment. The temperature was well over 100 degrees. After I finished servicing the equipment, I was wringing wet from perspiration, but this was Houston in the summertime.

Houston was my coming out city because I had more freedom. I had a lot more off-duty time there as compared to my previous assignments. It was a big city and although I did not have a car, there was a bus that ran from the base to the Third Ward, a section of the city where many of the Blacks lived. Texas Southern University was also in the Third Ward. Dowling street was the main drag. There were several clubs where we could go to hang out and meet the ladies. The base was located almost halfway between Galveston and Houston but it was easier for me to go to Houston because of the bus that ran from the base to the city.

While at Ellington, I attended Texas Southern University

(TSU) as an auditing (non - credit course) student. I took college algebra and English. At TSU, I met a young lady who was also auditing the math class as preparation to enter the University of Texas. She was to be one of the first Blacks to go to that school. I became very friendly with Jerry Ann Cannon because I used to study with her. Her father was very strict about allowing her to date but because I used to tutor her, he would allow me to stop by their home to visit. While I was attending TSU, I received my orders that re-assigned me to Germany. I had mixed emotions about this news. On the one hand, I was excited about going to Germany and on the other hand I was sorry to have to leave a lady whom I became very fond of. Although I only knew her for a short period of time, meeting her was the best part of my tour in Texas. We continued to write one another for a while. But as time passed the letters stopped. While in Germany, I lost track of her and always wondered what happened to her. For many years, I tried unsuccessfully to locate her. Some years later, I met someone who said she was a good friend of Jerry Ann and knew how to get in touch with her. This person told me that she was a widow living in the Washington, DC area. But for some reason, this lady reneged on her promise to provide me with the information. Later I learned that this person lied to me; she really did not know where Jerry lived.

After almost forty years, I finally ran into someone at the National Urban League Convention from Houston Texas who knew Jerry's sister. To my surprise, Jerry lived about two hours from me in Columbia Maryland. She was divorced from her second husband and was a doctor. She has a remarkable story to tell because she went to medical school at age 46 and completed her training to become a doctor. It was really good seeing her again and I was able to catch up on all of the details of what happened since the last time we had talked. This meeting brought closure to the question of what ever happened to Jerry

Ann. Sometimes, you go through life wondering "What If?" But I have learned that God has a plan for us and He brings people in and out of our lives for a reason. As I look back, meeting Jerry probably planted the seed of integrating a major university. She was one of the first Blacks to enter the University of Texas and a few years later, I was one of the first Blacks to attend the University of Virginia.

Although it was good seeing Jerry, I realized that the feelings I had for her some forty years ago were not the same. But it was important for me to bring closure to my quest of many years to find her. We agreed to stay in touch because although I was single at the time, I was in a long-term relationship. I realize then that God had provided me with the right person at the right time in my life. Sometimes we keep searching for something and learn that what we have been searching for has been right in front of us all the time.

Segregation Everywhere

In July 1956, I was shipped to Germany. I remember getting seasick on the ship on the second day out but afterwards everything was okay. We docked in Bremerhaven Germany and then boarded a train for our destination, Ramstein Air Force Base. Ramstein was a good base. We had maids to clean up our rooms and there was no more KP because the German civilians took care of all these duties. In fact, we ate off of real plates rather than those metal trays with compartments for your food that were typical in most mess halls. We also had semi-private rooms, which you only had to share with one or two people. The base had recreation facilities, an NCO club and an Officer's club. Again it had everything you needed except for women.

In Germany, my job code was changed. I was re-trained as a

microwave communications repairman. This was exciting for me because not only did I get a chance to go overseas but I was also expanding my knowledge in electronics. However, everything was not rosy in Germany for the Black serviceman. Some of the Germans would not associate with us. There were bars and other places in town where we were not welcomed. Part of the problem was some of the Germans still maintained their superior attitude from the days of Hitler. But some of the problems were brought about because of the racist attitudes of the White soldiers and airman who spread nasty rumors about Black men. These rumors started during World War II by White soldiers who told the Germans, for example, that Black men had tails that came out at night. Coming from the south, these attitudes were not new to me but I did not expect it to be so prevalent in Germany.

    I worked very hard to learn my new specialty. I always tried to be the best. I learned how to troubleshoot all types of problems and I would welcome the challenge of a new problem. In Germany, we worked shift work. A day shift ran from 7:00 AM to 5:00 PM and the night shift was from 5:00 PM to 7:00 AM. We would work a day shift then a night shift and then we would be off for two days. Each shift had a shift leader which usually was the highest ranking person on the shift or if everything else being equal, it was usually the most knowledgeable person on the shift. On my shift, I was both the highest ranking and the most knowledgeable but I was not made the shift leader. So I approached the sergeant in charge of the site and asked him if he was happy with my work. He said "absolutely," but he wanted to know why I asked the question. I said to him that obviously someone was not happy with me because I was passed over for shift leader. I also pointed out that I had noticed everyone who started with me had been promoted to staff sergeant and I was still an airman first class. "Why was this happening?" He said that he was not aware of this but he would check into it. To make a long story short, I was transferred to Siegelbach, another site not far away, and was made site chief and then later promoted to staff sergeant. That was the first time that I can ever remember speaking out against the system and it paid off.

As site chief at Siegelbach, I had some interesting challenges because I was the only Black on this site and I had a person reporting to me who felt he should have been site chief. In the military you follow orders, but I used some diplomacy with the guys on the site and everything worked out well. The first thing I did when I arrived at the site was to meet with the person, who wanted to be the site chief, to discuss his feelings. I told him that I understood that he might have been disappointed but that I needed his support. This was a good first step and we got along well. Additionally, some of the airmen were always late for shift change. I had the authority to discipline them for being late but I tried a different approach. I met with everyone and discussed the importance of being on time. I told them that being late was a habit and that we all have some good and bad habits. To help change their mindset, I made a big sign that read *"If you don't want to come on time, come early!"* It worked. My tour in Germany helped me develop my negotiation and team building skills which I would later need in the corporate world.

One of the things that came in handy was to learn how to speak German. It is important that you try to understand the culture and the language of the country that you are visiting. It is a good way to meet people, learn about their culture and to make friends. Many of the Germans were very curious about Black men. Oftentimes, if you would go into town they would stare at you. I remember an incident that happened when several of us traveled to Heidleberg to attend a festival. When the people arriving in town on buses saw us, they began pointing and staring at us. They obviously had not seen many Black people before. Once I was on the train and I started a conversation with a young lady who was very interested in learning more about Black people. She wanted to know why Black people came in so many shades of color. She asked me if my father or mother was white. I told her that my great grandfather was white and that was probably the reason I had a light brown complexion.

Black serviceman can tell you many interesting stories. One of the most interesting things happened to me in a bar in Mannheim. I saw a German lady who I was interested in meeting and when I tried to talk to her she said to me "I don't want to talk to a half white nigger because if I am going to be with a Black man I want a real Black man!" This surprised and crushed me because I was not ready for that. What I soon learned about German women was that they either dated white servicemen or Black servicemen but not both. There was segregation even dealing with the prostitutes. I did not like Germany as much as I liked the other countries I visited because some of the conditions and attitudes there reminded me of being in the states.

In 1957, I traveled to Berlin and had the opportunity to visit East Berlin before they put up the infamous wall. There were still restrictions when traveling between East and West Berlin. But at that time, East Berliners could visit and shop in West Berlin and vice versa. I went to East Berlin as part of a tour group. I remember walking down Stalin Alley, a main street in East Berlin. This Street was newly built but right behind it remained some of the rubble from the bombings of WWII that had ended some twelve years earlier. Stalin Alley was like a prop used for a play. It was a showcase street and a farce because on the streets directly behind it had rubble piled up from the bombings. The East Germans had never bothered to clean it up.

West Berlin on the other hand looked like an American city. It was very modern with plenty of shops and entertainment facilities. One of the most fascinating clubs that I visited was the Resi. It had telephones and a messaging system on each table. You could send a note to or call someone you wanted to meet. This was a great place to meet ladies if you could speak German. I had an opportunity to try out my German and to meet some very interesting "fraulines." I left Germany in 1958, and since that time they put up the Berlin Wall and in 2000 they tore it down. Maybe I will return to Germany one day to see the changes?

"Free at Last!" (Wonderful Copenhagen)

While in Germany, I had a chance to visit other countries. I visited Paris France, Amsterdam Holland and Copenhagen Denmark. I loved Copenhagen because the Danes are wonderful people. It was the first place that I had been where I truly felt welcomed. Copenhagen has a great amusement park called the Tivoli. It was a fun place to go to meet people. I had the opportunity to meet a young lady who made my stay in Copenhagen unforgettable. I met her family and I spent almost every day with her. I was told before I went to Denmark that many of the Danish women were attracted to Black men. I found that to be very true. I spent twenty days in Copenhagen and I had a ball.

Growing up in the south, I did not have the opportunity to date White women. But here it was too easy and I liked the way I was treated. I had never been treated with so much kindness, love and respect as I received in Copenhagen. For once I felt like a free man. I knew when the people looked at me it was oftentimes because they were interested in meeting me. People in Copenhagen did not automatically assume that I was an

American. As far as they were concerned, I could have been from Africa or one of the many countries whose inhabitants are dark skinned. So they would ask me in English "where are you from?" This was the first time that anyone ever asked. Most people in the U.S. and in Germany just assumed that I was an American Negro. Danish people wanted to learn more about me and to show me some hospitality. I fell in love with wonderful Copenhagen. *I felt that I had finally left the plantation!*

In 1957, America was having all kinds of problems integrating the schools. The Little Rock Arkansas incident was in all the papers in Europe. When people learned that I was from America, they would ask me what was going on in the states. They would ask why did I stay there and why not move to their country. I found myself defending America on the streets of Copenhagen. I told them that as bad as it might seem to them all the cities in America were not like Little Rock and it was still my home. I met some Black ex-servicemen who had elected to stay in Europe because they did not want to return to the states and deal with segregation. They said that they were happy there but many of them could not go home and take their wives and kids even if they wanted to do so. The laws in some states prohibited interracial marriages. They were stuck there, like it or not.

While in Denmark, I even considered staying there after I was discharged from the service. I also considered moving back to Europe after I completed college. I was caught up in that feeling of being free and being myself for a while. But reality set in for me after I returned home and became acclimated to the plantation life again. I knew I could escape the plantation but what about my family and friends? How would life be for them if I left them? I wanted to shut down the plantation because I knew in my heart that I would not be free if my family was not free too!

I was discharged from the Air Force on February 25, 1958, almost four years of duty to that date. After being in the Air force for four years, and then finding myself a civilian again caused mixed feelings for me. On one hand, I was happy to be out, but I had lost the security of having a job, a place to stay, and other benefits that I would have to worry about as a civilian. I did not want to return to the same life that I left four years ago. I was hoping that it would be different but I knew that I was returning to the old plantation. But I was a lot wiser and smarter. I knew that I would survive the plantation because I would not allow the system to keep me down.

Back Home to the Plantation

While in the Air Force, I had been accepted by Howard University Engineering School. But I had also applied to the University of Virginia and was waiting for my acceptance. I was able to get a job in the U.S. Post Office and worked there until I entered UVA in the following September. Working in the Post Office was considered a major coup because there was a long waiting list of people trying to get a job carrying mail. Although my father was just an elevator operator at the Post Office, he was well liked by everyone including the Postmaster. One day after I was discharged, my father mentioned to the Postmaster that I needed a job. So he told my father to tell me to take the test then let him know if I passed. Well passing the test was easy because as a veteran 10 points were automatically added to my score. So after I passed the test, my father told the postmaster and the next thing that I knew I was hired. I never told anyone how I got hired so quickly especially people who had waited for years to try to get hired.

Working at the post office was not an easy job. I was hired as a substitute carrier which meant I filled in when someone was sick or absent for whatever reason. My day started with helping sort the mail. Then, I would drive a truck to drop off mail at the various relay boxes so that the other postmen could pick up the additional mail when they arrived at that point on their route. When I finished that, I would go back to the office for my next assignment, which was typically delivering a part of a mail route on foot. I was given very explicit instructions that I could walk as fast as I wanted, but don't come back to the office until a specific time. Each route was timed and they did not want some rookie coming in and messing up the system.

When I finished delivering mail, I had to checkout a truck to travel around the city to collect mail from mailboxes. This effort took approximately four hours. In and out of the truck, scooping up the mail from the boxes, putting the mail into the appropriate bag and making certain it had the right tag on it. If the mail was improperly tagged, you received a demerit. I worked approximately 12 hours a day earning $2.00 an hour, which was real good pay for 1958 in Richmond. I worked at Post office for approximately five months and during that period I lost over twenty pounds. I literally worked my butt off.

One final note on my post office experience. As I mentioned, working at the post office was a big deal in Richmond. Once you got on there, you stayed until you retired. There were a number of college graduates including former schoolteachers working at the post office because it was the highest paying job available to most Blacks. So when I announced that I was leaving the post office to go to college, a number of people told me that I was making a mistake leaving a "good" job.

Even the superintendent of mails approached me after I turned in my resignation. He said "AJ, I understand you are leaving the post office to go to college?" "That's Right!" I said. "What school will you be attending?" "The University of

Virginia." "You mean Virginia Union University don't you? (The Black School)." I said "No sir, UVA." He gave me a puzzled look because he didn't think that Blacks went to UVA (and he was right because I was the only Black undergraduate to enter UVA in 1958). Then he asked what was my major, and I told him Engineering. Finally, he asked: "Do you feel engineering is better than the post office?" I could not believe he asked me this question but he was obviously proud of working at the post office and I learned never to burn any bridges. So I said: *"Sir, if you like the post office, nothing can be better."* And that was the best *no answer* I could give because I knew that I might want to carry mail at Christmas time to earn some extra money. Again, you do not want to burn your bridges because you never know when you might need to come that way again. As it turned out, I did deliver mail at Christmas a couple of times after I left the post office.

A Goal
by Aubrey B. Jones, Jr.

A *goal* is something
that you want to do

It should be challenging, measurable
and achievable too.

A *goal* is something
that you believe you can do.

And you should write it down
and keep it in view.

One *goal* or two, many or few,
you make that call.

But too many *goals* are almost as bad
as no *goals* at all!

A goal is something you want to do. Your goal can be anything. For example, you could have a goal to find a job, to graduate from school, to get your GED, or to learn how to use a computer. Goals should be specific, measurable and have a deadline-a due date.

III Life on Mr. Jefferson's Plantation - UVA

The Missing Application

I became interested in attending the University of Virginia (UVA) for several reasons. First, it was the best School I could afford to attend. As a Virginia resident, my tuition was relatively low especially compared to students from out of the state. The second reason was I knew someone who was already there, Rupert Picot, and he encouraged me to come to the school. UVA had an excellent engineering school. I knew that there were not many Blacks attending UVA, and I did not know whether or not they would accept me. When I submitted my application, I was stationed in Germany. I wanted to enter UVA during mid year but the admissions office told me that they only accepted first year students in September. So I requested to be considered for the next class which was September 1958.

After I was discharged I learned that I had to take the college entrance examination which is now called the SAT. I studied very hard for the exam. But after I took it, I heard nothing from UVA. So I called the Admissions Office to check on my status and to my surprise they told me that they had no record of me applying to UVA. I was really upset because now it was April, and I did not know what I would be doing in September. Although I already had an acceptance from Howard University, I did not like what was happening. Naturally, I assumed that someone did not want me to attend the school and conveniently lost my application.

I told Rupert what had happened and he suggested that I come to Charlottesville and speak to the Dean of the Engineering School. So I drove to UVA and met with Dean Lawrence Quarles who was a very gracious person. To my surprise, he told me that I had already been accepted to the School of Engineering but he could not explain why the Admissions Office said that it had no record of my application. He did call Admissions, while I was sitting in his office, and straighten out the situation. He was very apologetic for the inconvenience that UVA had caused me and he assured me that he was looking forward to seeing me in September. I felt really good after that meeting.

Six Things You Can Do *To Get Ahead*...

1	Be Inquisitive (Ask Question)
2	Be Smart (Don't Follow the Crowd)
3	Think Positive (It Will Give You Power)
4	Be Confident (Say "Yes I Can!")
5	Be Diligent (Do Your Best)
6	Set Goals (Know Where You Are Going)

I Can Do It Too!

For a Black attending UVA in 1958 was a major event. I felt proud and excited about being accepted to UVA – *"Mr. Jefferson's University."* My family and friends were proud but I was also very apprehensive. I kept telling myself *"I can do it"* and if for some reason I did not make it, it would not be because I didn't try. In addition to Rupert Picot, there were other Black students who were enrolled at the University. A number of Black students who had enrolled ahead of me were not there when I enrolled. My friend, Rupert, was not there either. Many left because they were either unwilling or unable to put up with the pressure of being one of the first Blacks to attend a southern white school. When some Black people learned that I was going to UVA, they said to me "why are you going to UVA, you know can't make it there!" Others said *"don't go there and embarrass us!"*

Many of the Black students felt the pressure of having to succeed. We felt pressure from family, friends, ministers and teachers. It was as though we had the weight of the Black community on our shoulders. If we failed, we felt that it would not only be a bad reflection on ourselves but it might keep other Blacks from attending UVA. We were in the spotlight and under a microscope by both the Black and white communities. I put additional pressure on myself. Every quiz was a final exam to me. I don't believe I could have made it at UVA right out of high school. The four years in the Air Force definitely help give me the maturity and toughness needed to survive the pressures at UVA. There were also a number of people who encouraged and supported me and I thank them for that. But as a 23-year-old veteran, I was much more mature than the average student at UVA. I was better prepared mentally to handle the stress. I had a mission, I was focused and nobody was going to stop me!

As a first year student, I had to go to school a week earlier than the rest of the students. Freshmen week was uneventful but one thing happened that made me feel welcomed. When I went to the dining room, I sat at a table by myself. Many of the students stared at me but one student, Gary Cuozzo, asked if he could sit with me. I did not know it at the time but he was a quarterback on the football team, I believe he was from New Jersey. His warm reception helped me feel a little more comfortable in the dining room. Other students on my dormitory hall also stopped by the room to introduce themselves. Basically things went well for me during the first week.

Dean Quarles met with all of the first year engineering students and he asked everyone, who was either a Valedictorian or Salutatorian at his high school, to raise his hand. Over half of the 250 students raised their hands. He made the point that we were all good students in high school otherwise we would not have been accepted to UVA. But he admonished us that our high school record did not mean a thing from this point on. He told us that we had to prove ourselves all over again. He put everything in perspective for us.

One thing was made very clear to all of us. UVA, Mr. Jefferson's School, was steeped in tradition. It was an all-male school, coats and ties were worn to class and there was an honor system. And being one of the few Black students, I was not about to start breaking tradition. Hearing about the great traditions of UVA, I was in awe when I walked around the grounds (as the campus was called). Looking at the magnificent architecture and thinking about the history, made me feel proud. "The Rotunda and the Lawn were ever-present reminders of the traditions of honor, responsibility and gentlemanly conduct exemplified by Mr. Jefferson and his University." And I must admit I liked the prestige of being a student there.

I put a lot of pressure on myself because I wanted to do well. But after being out of high school for five years before going back to college, it was a real challenge. I did okay with my math but chemistry and a course called Descriptive Geometry, which was a course where you had to visualize things in 3 dimensions, were my real challenges. I was able to get a tutor after mid-term for chemistry but I failed the second half of the Descriptive Geometry Course. One of the things I did not take in high school was drafting. If I had taken it, I would probably have had an easier time with visualizing things in 3D.

I had no social life during my first year of college. Most of my time was spent studying. One of my problems was I did not know how to study in college. I put the time in but I did not get the return for my investment of time. A Black PHD candidate in Chemistry, Mr. Arthur Walls, tutored me in Chemistry. He taught me how to understand rather than try to memorize a bunch of formulas. Because of his help, my grade went from failing at mid term to a final grade of a "'B." Mr. Walls had taught me science in the 9th grade at Armstrong High School. Despite the problems he was having at UVA (with his racist professor) trying to earn his Doctorate, he took time out to help me and I will never forget him for that.

Because my score on the entrance exam was not high enough in English, I was required to take remedial English. My first reaction was that I did not need to take this non-credit course. I felt that I could pass English 101 without taking this remedial course. So I pleaded my case to the head of the English department and requested that I be allowed to take English 101. Surprisingly, I was able to convince him that I would be able to pass English 101 without taking remedial English. After I received approval to take English 101, I learned that I could not fit the class into my schedule which was already set. So I swallowed my pride and took the remedial English course. At first, I was embarrassed because I was the only Black in the class taking this non credit course in the evening. But it was needed (and deep down I knew it). It provided me the foundation I needed for English 101, and it helped me in subsequent courses.

During one of my English classes, we had a writing assignment and I said to my professor, "I know what I want to say but I don't know how to say it." He said to me, "that's a lot of bull." If you know what you want to say, just say it! Don't worry about using the right words, spelling or grammar. Just write down your thoughts as fast as you can. He told me to use "placeholders" for my thoughts until I was able to come up with the right words. This suggestion helped me get over writer's block. At that time, my vocabulary consisted of a lot of slang. In fact, I told my professor that I had a large vocabulary but it was all slang. He smiled, and said, "That's a start." Over the years, I made an effort to increase my vocabulary. Anytime I came across a word I did not understand, I looked it up in the dictionary. Even after graduation, I kept a list of new words and tried to learn a new word a day.

One of the benefits of attending this class was that I met Professor Luther Gore. He was only three years older than I, and was very open minded and supportive. I felt comfortable talking to him. In fact, several of the professors of the English Department including Graham Hereford and Alan Gianinny were favorites because of their open-mindedness and overall support. One of the strengths of UVA's engineering program was its English department. They stressed the importance of being able to communicate effectively which proved to be one of the keys to my success in the corporate world. Not only am I able to write specifications, business plans and other documents but I am also the author of ten books on computers. I attribute a lot of this success to UVA's English department. One of the lessons

I learned was that no matter how good your engineering and/or computer skills might be, you must be able to communicate. *My engineering degree helped me get the job but my communications skills got me promoted!*

My roommate Robert "Bobby" Bland, was a senior. They put all of the Black students together and I guess because I was the oldest of the undergraduates they made us roommates. But that was a blessing because Bobby was majoring in electrical engineering also. He was able to give me the scoop on all of the professors. Some of the professors were known to give the brothers a hard time so we would try to avoid them if we could. That was pretty easy to do because the Dean's office knew these professors. So if you were a Black student and if there was another section available, all you had to do was to go see "Dean Jean" and she would make the necessary changes. "Dean Jean's" name was Jean Holiday who was Dean Quarles Administrative assistant. But as everyone knew, *"Dean Jean"* ran the office. She was very helpful to all of the students and especially to the Black students.

There was one math professor who I was told to avoid because he had been identified as a racist. But I needed the course, Differential Equations, and his class was the only one available. Everyone told me that I would flunk that course so I took the course expecting the worse. To my surprise, I did not have any major problems in his class. In fact, he was an excellent teacher who did an outstanding job of breaking down the lessons and making them clear. He was also very entertaining. For example, someone would ask him how to solve a particular problem and he would draw a very small box on the blackboard and say "this should be enough space to solve this problem." He was reputed to be very wealthy (I was told that he worked for $1 a year) and to be the head of the Virginia States Rights

Association. Also, I believe he had a law degree. Nevertheless, I really enjoyed his class.

During the final exam, I was struggling to complete my exam on time and I was the last one left in the class. He told me to take my time and that he would wait until I was finished. At the end of the exam, I said, "*Professor Janus* I don't know whether or not this is ethical but I just want to tell you that I thoroughly enjoyed your class." And he said, "Thank you Mr. Jones, it must be unethical because no one ever told me that before." We both laughed and I left. I also passed differential equations. I did not want *Professor Janus* to think that I was trying to "brown nose" him but I wanted him to know that I really thought he was an excellent teacher. One lesson I learned here was that in spite of his reputation, *Professor Janus* treated me with respect and did not bring politics into the classroom. He did not have to like me as long as he respected me.

Behind the Scenes

Most of the custodians, cooks and maintenance people at the university were Black. Many of them had worked at UVA for years and they were very happy to see Black students finally attend the university. They would tell us who they thought were the most racist professors based on their experience. It was surprising how much information a maid or janitor could pick up. Especially when some Whites assumed that they were too ignorant to understand what they were saying. It reminds me of how the slave masters on the plantations used to treat the house servants. They talked openly about many things because they thought that their servants were too dumb to understand what was being said. One maid in particular at the engineering school was very helpful to us. She always wanted to know how we were doing. She would check the grades when they were posted on the bulletin board. She was interested in our welfare and always offered words of encouragement.

There was one benefit that we had by knowing the maid. Some evenings after dinner, we would go back to the engineering school to get a classroom so that we could use the blackboard to work out problems. But rooms were a premium and you had to get there early to reserve a room unless you knew the maid. All we had to do was to let her know that we needed a classroom and she would reserve one for us and then locked the door until we were ready to use it. That allowed us time to take a brief nap after dinner and then be ready to study the rest of the night. Another benefit was that all of the cooks and the servers in the dining room were Black and we always got an extra helping of food. We had an extended family at UVA pulling for us to make it. Many of the Black workers were perhaps living vicariously through us and seeing us there made them feel proud too!

Bobby Bland also played another important role in my life. He introduced me to my wife, Alyce. At the time we met, I did not know she was going to be my wife. In fact, she told me later that she did not even like me at first. She thought that I was conceited. I met her during my first year of college and did not see her again until my third year because she left Charlottesville to attend a business school in Cleveland Ohio. Charlottesville was a small college town with a very small Black community. Many of the Blacks in the town worked at the university in some capacity. Some of the Black students were young enough to date high school students. Because I was older, there were only a few single young women who lived in town. When we had our parties, oftentimes we would invite some of the young schoolteachers or student teachers. But most of the time I would have to go home to Richmond, which was 70 miles away, if I wanted to date someone. After Alyce returned to Charlottesville, that all changed. We became very good friends. She was very supportive of me. She typed my term papers, invited me down for dinner and was someone I could talk to when I was feeling down. Her mother, Mrs. Alice Brown, also was very good to me. Mrs. Brown became a second mother to me and we still remained close even after Alyce's death in 1985.

The Blacks are Coming! The Blacks are Coming!

There was a widely held misconception that integration at UVA began in the early 1970s. But integration happened some 20 years earlier. In 1950, Gregory Swanson, a 26-year-old lawyer from Danville, Virginia, challenged UVA's right to continue the practice of segregation. In doing so, he challenged the law of the Commonwealth of Virginia which forbade "race mixing" in tax supported schools. Mr. Swanson took his case to court with the support of the NAACP and won his suit. There was some publicity surrounding his suit but nothing like the problems at "Ole Miss," "University of Alabama" and the "University of Georgia." A book entitled *"The Desegregated Heart"* written by Sarah Patton Boyle tells the story of Mr. Swanson's suit and later admittance to UVA. Mrs. Boyle was the wife of a professor at the university who personally crusaded for his admittance. Although Mr. Swanson was admitted to UVA, he did not live on the University grounds; he had to live in a Black hotel in town. It is my understanding that he attended UVA for about a year to take additional course work since he already had his law degree from Howard University. Even though Mr. Swanson did not graduate from UVA, he helped pave the way for Dr. Walter N. Ridley who was the first Black to graduate from UVA in 1953. And in 1959, Bobby Bland was the first Black undergraduate to obtain a degree from UVA.

UVA's integration started before the modern civil rights era. Dr. Walter N. Ridley received his doctorate degree in education in 1953 before the U.S. Supreme Court ruled in 1954 that segregated schools were unlawful. This was before Martin Luther King organized the bus boycott in Montgomery Alabama in 1956. It was before James Meredith integrated the University of Mississippi in 1961 and before Charlene Hunter broke down the barriers at the University of Georgia.

Here is a bit of history. All of the first Black undergraduates were engineering students since none of the Black Colleges in the State of Virginia offered an engineering curriculum. Prior to 1954, any Black resident who wanted to take a curriculum that was not offered at a Black college in Virginia, the state of Virginia would pay for that student to attend any out-of-state school of his or her choice. Many Blacks took full advantage of this free education and enrolled in northern schools and obtained their degrees. This applied to all degrees not offered by a Black college in Virginia. After the U.S. Supreme Court's decision of 1954, Brown versus the Board of Education, Virginia had to admit Blacks into white colleges. Initially, UVA admitted Blacks for courses that were not offered at the Black Schools, such as Engineering, Law and Medicine. In the early fifties, there were some students who entered at the graduate level in Law (Swanson), Education (Ridley) and Medicine (Edward Wood and Edward Nash) but the undergraduate schools were still segregated.

In 1955, the first undergraduates were admitted to the School of Engineering: Robert Bland of Petersburg, George Harris of Lynchburg and Ted Thomas of Chesapeake Va. In the following year, Harold Marsh and Rupert Picot Jr. both of Richmond entered the School of Engineering. Four first year Black students were admitted to the engineering school in 1957: Walter Payne Jr. of Charlottesville, Nathaniel Gatlin of Petersburg, Elmer Dandridge and James Trice both from Richmond. In 1958, I entered engineering school and John Merchant was the first Black to finish UVA's Law School. In 1959, Leroy Willis entered

UVA and my roommate, Robert Bland, was the first Black undergraduate to finish with a Bachelor of Electrical Engineering degree. In 1960, after a year in engineering school, Leroy Willis decided to challenge the system. Until then, undergraduate Blacks at UVA were only allowed to attend Engineering School. Being able to attend the College of Arts and Sciences had been denied to Black Students in spite of the 1954 ruling of the Supreme Court that all schools were to desegregate "with all deliberate speed." UVA had decided to remain with the old law of "separate but equal," until Leroy Willis decided to challenge the University's adherence to the "separate but equal" law. In 1960, Leroy was quietly allowed into the college. He transferred from the Engineering School and switched his major from Chemical Engineering to Chemistry. Leroy also had the privilege of opening another door. He was the first Black to live on the Lawn in 1961.

To live in one of the prestigious "Lawn" rooms is considered an honor at the university. Located in Mr. Jefferson's original buildings, these rooms are truly in the center of the University. The Lawn, anchored at the north end by the Rotunda, still looks and functions much as it did in Jefferson's era—as a vital community organized around learning. Each side of the lawn has five pavilions and a number of student rooms located between them. The Lawn's ten pavilions are each unique. Jefferson wanted the buildings to do triple duty—besides functioning as classrooms and faculty living quarters; each embodies classical design features that make it a fitting subject for architectural study.

The Lawn is a beautiful setting, probably the most popular place for students to relax, study, and play. In 1961, the Lawn was only available to students who were top achievers. These rooms were furnished with a bed, desk, wardrobe, bookcase, rocking chair, and blinds on the windows. Additionally, most rooms had a fireplace. No air conditioning, kitchen, computer rooms, or study lounges were available. Despite the lack of a number of 21st century amenities, many students applied for the limited number of rooms on the Lawn. Leroy enjoyed the prestige of living on the Lawn except when he had to go outside of his room, during the winter, to use the bathroom which was located behind the rooms on the Lawn.

Leroy and others were the real pioneers. Because they blazed the trail, it was a little bit easier for me in 1958. I did not suffer as many of the racial slurs or insulting signs hanging on the dorms because by the time I was admitted Blacks had been on campus for several years. There were times when many of us thought about quitting or giving up but we couldn't do that because there was too much at stake. We couldn't let all those people down who were pulling for us to make it. But most importantly, we couldn't let ourselves down. So we stayed and helped each other. We relied on each other for strength and support. Harold Marsh said it best, *"Because Bobby Bland stayed, I stayed. Because I stayed, Elmer Dandridge and James Trice stayed. Because they stayed, Aubrey stayed."* Because we all stayed, others stayed and we now have a rich Black heritage that's still growing at UVA.

The No-Name Fraternity

The social life of the University was centered primarily on fraternity life. If you were not in or allowed to be in a fraternity, opportunities for socializing were few. As expected, the doors to fraternity life and other social clubs were closed to Blacks. Oftentimes people asked me if I belong to a fraternity and I would usually answer that there were no Black fraternities at UVA. Later, I thought about my answer and realized that *I did* belong to a fraternity. It was not formally organized. It was not incorporated, it had no secret rites, no secret hand shakes and it *did not have a name*. But it was a group of brothers who were bound together with a common purpose, a common interest and a common cause. We had to do it for survival. We did everything together. We studied together, shared each others pain together, went to church together and partied together. *"Sounds like a fraternity to me!"* Sometimes after a rough exam, we would take a break. We would all gather in one of the brother's room and put on some music and just talk, tell some jokes and tell some lies too. We had fun! Occasionally, we would go to town if we knew of a party. Some of the young Black men in town did not like the UVA students because we had a "semi-celebrity" status, which appealed to the young ladies in town and their parents. But the young Brothers saw us as coming in to take their women. There were occasional fights but nothing real serious.

There was a really nice place outside of town we could go to party called Bren-Wanna. But the truth is that we really did not have a lot of time to party anywhere. Only two White restaurants in town served Black students, *The University Cafeteria* (Not affiliated with UVA) and the *Virginian*. These places were located near the campus, on a strip of Main Street, called "The Corner." But Black residents of Charlottesville could not eat in these places unless they were with a Black student. My roommate, Jim Trice, reminded me that when the *Virginian* was sold, the new management refused to serve him and another student. Such was life in Charlottesville. We could still eat on the campus in UVA's cafeteria, located in Newcomb Hall, however.

On weekends, when families and friends visited the campus, many were surprised to see Black students there. When we walked into the cafeteria, sometimes the people would stop eating for a second and stare at us. It was a strange feeling because before we walked into the cafeteria, you could hear the buzzing of people talking. But, for one instant, the noise level would drop several decibels when they spotted us. And you could almost read the lips of some of them saying, "I didn't know that Negroes went here."

There were several big weekends on the grounds (campus) when the White fraternities had their parties. They imported women from nearby women's colleges (since UVA was an all-male school then). Of course, Blacks were not invited to these parties. So we would plan our parties around the big weekends so that we would have something to do. There were families in Charlottesville that opened up their homes to us so that we could have a place to relax and enjoy ourselves. Theresa Walker and Dr. "Punjab" Jackson's homes were two of our favorite hangouts. On several of the big weekends, we attended the concerts that were held in the gym, (if they had someone we wanted to hear). We would also invite women from out of town. I remember inviting a lady from Richmond for a weekend. She had to stay with one of the families in town because there were no suitable hotels for her. That weekend, we attended the concert, went to a party and then back to the books.

One of the things the *No-Name fraternity* did was to save old exams, reports and homework assignments so that we could pass them down to those who followed us. The White fraternity brothers had access to much more information but it was a start for us. The university had a very strict honor code. And if you cheated, lied or stole you could be kicked out of school. Each student had to write the following pledge on all exams and other work as designated by the professor: *"On my honor I have neither given nor received aid on this exam"* and then sign it. The professors usually handed out the exams and then left the room because they did not have to worry about anyone cheating.

Black students had to be very careful that no one accused them of cheating. It only took two students to accuse you and then you would have to go before the honor committee to defend yourself. We were all paranoid about this system because if two racist white students wanted to swear that you were cheating on a test, they could do so. Fortunately, it never happened. But one of the things *The No-name Fraternity* warned new students about was to never put yourself in a position where there could be the slightest reason for someone to accuse you. For example, I would always sit up front and made certain that there was nothing around me that would even look suspicious. So in addition to trying to study and pass an exam, you had to worry about making certain that you were above reproach.

UVA had a reputation of a hard drinking school. So Harold Marsh gave us some survival tips on attending sporting events. One of the things he told us was that if we go to a football game to beware of an impromptu playing of "Dixie." When the band played "Dixie" most of the spectators would stand and sing along. He told us that we should not stand. In 1958, UVA did not have a very good football team as I recall. But the band still played "Dixie" and the drunken spectators also sang, "I think we need another drink for the glory of UVA." Mix "Dixie" and "Drunks" and you have a formula for problems. But fortunately for me, there was only one isolated incident that occurred at a football game. As I recall, Jim Trice and I were sitting in the stands and the band played "Dixie." Most of the spectators stood but Jim and I did not stand. One drunk spotted us and yelled "There they go, two N _____." Interestingly, nobody laughed at what he said and just looked at him as if they were saying to him, "shut up and sit down!" He did not get the response from the crowd that he was hoping for, so he shut up and sat down. What a relief and perhaps a sign that a change in attitudes by the majority of the people was taking place.

Charter Members of UVA's No-Name Fraternity
(Undergraduate Chapter)

Name	Year Admitted	Degree & Year Graduated
Robert "Bobby" Bland	1955	BSEE 1959
George Harris	1955	
Ted Thomas	1955	
Harold Marsh	1956	BSEE 1960
Rupert Picot	1956	
Elmer Dandridge	1957	BSEE 1962
Nathaniel Gatlin	1957	
Walter Payne Jr.	1957	
James Trice	1957	BSCHE 1963
Aubrey Jones Jr.	1958	BSEE 1963
Leroy Willis	1959	BSCHEM 1962
Wesley Harris	1960	BSAE 1964
Charles Yancey	1960	BSCE 1964
Douglas Roundtree	1960	
Edwin Williams	1960	BSCHEM 1965
Andrew Hocker	1961	

In Memory of Harold M. Marsh, Sr. (1938-1997)

On July 23, 1997, Harold Marsh was tragically shot to death by an unknown assailant while his car was stopped at a traffic light in Richmond, Va. Harold was a Richmond Attorney and a substitute judge.

Harold was the second Black student to earn an undergraduate degree from UVA. In the engineering school, he was the first Black to earn Intermediate Honors, to make the Dean's List every semester, to become a member of the electrical engineering honor society, Eta Kappa Nu, and to be recognized in Who's Who in Electrical Engineering. He stood as a significant influence on me and other Black engineering students who came after him.

The Struggle Makes You Stronger

More good things happened to me than bad while at UVA. It was a little easier for me because Bobby, Harold and Elmer preceded me. But I still remember how some people reacted when they saw us on campus. I mentioned earlier that at a football game someone yelled obscenities at my roommate and me. But that was nothing compared to what a professor did to me. I failed a course, Descriptive Geometry, during my first year. So I took the course again the next year. The final exam was valued at 50% of my total grade. I had a passing grade going into the final but I had to pass the final exam. I ended up with a 73 total and 75 was passing. The reason, I failed was because there was a problem which I felt I was graded unfairly.

Typically, if you only needed a couple of points to pass, the professor would usually give the student the benefit of the doubt. This was especially true if you were taking a course that was not a prerequisite for any other course and if you were taking it a second time like I was. So when I questioned the professor about my grade, he would not change it. And I said to him, "you mean to tell me that you are going to fail me a second time with a 73." He said, *"If it will make you feel any better, I will lower your grade and flunk you with a lower score!"*

I was really upset with this guy, and I had to restrain myself, to keep from punching him, but I did not want to get kicked out of school. At that point in my life, I did not cry very easily but I went to the field behind the physics building and just ran around the field with tears streaming down my face. I had to let off some steam because I was about to explode.

The next day, I went to see the head of the department to plead my case. Interestingly, he agreed with my interpretation of the problem but said he could not change my grade. But he did make a good suggestion. He told me that I should just forget about that course for now because it was not a prerequisite for any of the courses I had to take. He told me to concentrate on my other courses and then take this course later. He also offered encouragement by telling me that I had done well to have only failed one course because over 50% of the engineering students either flunk out or transfer to another major during the first two years. I felt a little better and followed his suggestion and took the course again during my final semester, two and a half years later. But this story does not end here.

During my last semester at UVA, the course I failed was one of the three courses I needed for graduation. So when I signed up for the course I made certain I did not get the same professor whom I had twice before. In fact, my professor was now the same head of the department who had given me the good advice. But as my luck would have it, my professor became very ill. And guess who I got as my professor again? You got it! But I made up my mind that this course was not going to keep me from graduating. There was also a rumor that if you failed a course three times that you could not get a degree from UVA. I don't know if that was true or not but no way was I going to fail this course again. I went into the final exam with an "A" average and my final grade was a "C." But it didn't matter anymore because I was out of there. *I was graduating with Praise – "Thank You Lordy!"*

UVA was a microcosm of the real world that I would have to face after graduation. The lesson I learned from this incident is that life is full of obstacles and challenges and if you give up every time you are faced with a challenge, you'll never accomplish anything. **I learned the struggle makes you stronger!**

Blacks Who Attended UVA During Period 1950-1963*

* This list does not include all Blacks who attended UVA during this period. A few unidentified students attended UVA for special studies in education for a short period of time.

Blacks Who Attended UVA During Period 1950-1963*

Date	Names	Remarks
1950	Gregory Swanson	First to enter Law school but dropped out in the summer 1951
1953 (Jun)	**Dr. Walter Ridley**	First Black to gain a degree of any kind at UVA and also first Black to earn a doctorate at a major white southern university
1953 (Aug)	**Dr. E. Louise Stokes-Holmes**	First Black woman to earn a degree at UVA
1953	Edward B. Nash Edward T. Wood	First two Blacks to enter UVA's Medical School.
1954	Albert H. Luck Hannibal E. Howell	3rd & 4th Blacks to enter UVA's Medical School
1955	Anna Franklin-Savage	First Black woman to enter UVA's Med School
1955	**Robert Bland** "1st Black Undergraduate, 1959"	One of 1st Black undergraduates to enter UVA's engineering school. land stayed on and **became the 1st Black under - graduate from UVA.**
1955	George Harris Theodore Thomas	Two of three first undergraduates to enter UVA. Dropped out in 1956
1955	**John Merchant** "1st Law School's Graduate"	Entered law school in 1955 and **the first graduate from Law School in 1958.**
1956	Isaac Hunt	Third Black to enter Law school **and the second to graduate in 1959.**
1956	Harold Marsh & Rupert Picot	Rupert dropped out in 1957 **and Harold was the 2nd to graduate from Engineering** School in 1960.
1957	Elmer Dandridge James Trice Nathaniel Gatlin Walter Payne	Entered engineering school. **Elmer graduated in 1962 with BSEE, Jim Trice graduated in 1963 with BSCHE,** Gatlin dropped out and Walter Payne transferred to another University.
1957	William Womack Clint Murchison	6th & 7th Blacks to enter Med School. **They graduated in 1961.**

Date	Names	Remarks
1958	Aubrey Jones	Only Black undergraduate to enter UVA in 1958. **Earned BSEE in 1963**. 1st Black Veteran to graduate from UVA.
1958	Arthur A Walls	Entered a Doctoral Program in Chemistry. My tutor in Chemistry during my first year. "I would not have passed that course without his help!" (Aubrey Jones)
1959	**A. Leroy Willis** "1st to Desegregate the College" "1st to live on the Lawn"	Transferred from Norfolk State to UVA's engineering school. In 1960, he was allowed to enter the College. He Majored in Chemistry and **graduated in 1962**. He also had the privilege of becoming the first black to live on the Lawn.
1960	**Wesley Harris** "The Scholar"	Wesley was the first Black to earn a degree in **aeronautical engineering in 1964. First man (black or white) to complete engineering honors program**. Second Black to live on the Lawn (1963-64); 1st Black to desegregate the Jefferson Literary and Debating Society.
1960	Charles Yancey	First Black to graduate with a **Civil Engineering Degree (1964)**
1960	Douglas Roundtree	Did not graduate.
1960	Edwin Williams	Second undergraduate to enter the College of Arts and Sciences. Majored in Chemistry (1965)
1960	Virginius Thornton	Candidate for a doctoral program but did not graduate.
1961	Andrew Hocker	Did not graduate
1962	Barbara Starks Favazza "1st Black Woman to Graduate from Medical School"	2nd Black woman to enter Med School **and 1st to graduate in 1966**
1963	Vivian W. Pinn	3rd Black woman to enter Med School. Graduated in 1967

Anger
By Aubrey B. Jones, Jr.

    If it is to be; it's up to me
    I *control* my anger before it controls me

I can't control the things that anger me
I can't control the people who bother me
I can't control the circumstances in my life
I can't control the struggles and the strife
But I can control what I do or say
I can control how I approach each day
I *control* what my reaction will be
I *control* my anger before it controls me
    (Chorus)
Anger is a completely normal healthy emotion
But controlling it is more than a notion
It varies from mild irritation to intense fury and rage
Uncontrolled, It can occur at any time and at any age
When it gets out of control and turns very destructive
It can lead to problems and be very disruptive
Sometimes I feel that I've just had enough
But I refuse to react negatively to all that stuff
I *control* what my reaction will be
I *control* my anger before it controls me
    (Chorus)

When I feel the anger developing inside
Sometimes I just take it in stride
But holding anger inside can cause problems you see
Because I need to release the pressure inside of me
I don't yell or scream or push anyone around
I just try to relax and calm myself down
I take deep breaths and count to ten
I think pleasant thoughts and count again
I *control* what my reaction will be
I *control* my anger before it controls me

> If it is to be; it's up to me
> I *control* my anger before it controls me

The "Rat Pack"

One interesting experience for me while at UVA was my study group. During my third and fourth years at UVA, I joined a study group comprised of four other guys and myself. Four of us were veterans and everyone except me was married. Although I was the only Black in the group, we hit it off well. Because we were older than the typical students, we had one thing in common.-"we were there to study not to party." We were very focused. We jokingly called ourselves the "Rat Pack" because there were four Whites and one Black, like Sammy Davis, Jr.; Frank Sinatra et al – The original "Rat Pack."

Bill was my lab partner for most of the electronics labs. Since both of us were electronic technicians in the U.S Air Force, the labs were very easy for us. I believe Bill and I started to study together first, and then Bob, Jim and Larry joined the group later. I felt that Bill's and my value to the group was that we brought some practical experience. It is one thing to solve a theoretical problem but it's another thing to understand how solving a problem fits into the greater scheme of things.

Bill was a nice guy; he was very open and honest with me. Although we did not discuss it a lot, Bill knew the challenges that I had at UVA. He lived off campus and on several occasions he invited me to his home for dinner. I did not socialize with the other members outside of the group's study sessions. Bill graduated in 1962 and I graduated six months later in February 1963. Both he and I moved to the Philadelphia area after graduation and we stayed in touch for a while.

The lesson learned from this study group was similar to the lesson that I learned in the Air Force. You cannot say "all Whites or all Blacks do this or that." You have to judge people on their merits. Christians are taught, however, "to hate the sin but love the sinner." I don't want to imply that I am totally there yet, but I'm working on it. Although the study group readily accepted me, they did not openly embrace my roommate, Elmer.

I brought Elmer to one of the sessions because he wanted some help with a subject that we were covering. Initially, they did not object to Elmer being there. But Elmer ended up with a higher grade on the test than several of them and they did not like it. So some members of the group said to me that Elmer did not add value to the group. They said that he just listened, and did not actively participate in the discussions. In other words they were calling him a "leech." Because Elmer was quiet, they underestimated him. But when they found out that he was a bright young man who just needed a little help they did not want to help him. Elmer attended a few more sessions but he felt uncomfortable. I considered quitting the study group because of their attitude towards Elmer. But I didn't. I continued to study with the group and then I would help Elmer when he needed it.

One of the lessons I learned was that some whites will accept you and talk to you but they will not accept other Blacks. Sometimes they might even say to you that "you're different." Now I don't know if the members of the "Rat Pack" felt this way because it was never mentioned to me. I do remember times when a student might speak to me in class but if he saw me on "The Corner" or off campus he would not bother to speak. As a result, I learned not to let it bother me if someone did not want to speak to me. It was his problem and not mine!

Putting a Little Light on the Subject

There were some other benefits to attending UVA aside from the basic educational values. It prepared me for the corporate environment where I would have to deal with biased opinions and myths about Blacks. Myths spread by Whites who did not even know you but assumed that they knew everything about you. At UVA, I had the opportunity to talk to a number of White students and to get a better understanding of how they felt about certain issues. I remember sitting in one of the study rooms in my dormitory when I overheard some White students discussing what was wrong with "colored people." They had no idea that I was in the building much less that I could hear what they were saying. I tried to ignore the conversation until they started making statements like "all colored people are inferior, they steal and have no moral values and so on." I could not resist the temptation to see who was doing all this talking and quoting statistics like he was an expert on colored people.

The door to the room where they were having this discussion was open, so I went to the room and knocked on the door and said *"Excuse me but I could not help from overhearing your discussion, perhaps I can put a little light on the subject?"* There was silence and an embarrassed look from the guy who was doing all the talking. So I continued by saying that you are certainly entitled to your opinions. But "Where are you getting all the statistics from that you are using?" And by the way, may I ask, "where do you live?"

To my surprise, he said Richmond. "Richmond" I said. I live in Richmond and I know what you are saying is not true. Further, I said, even if all of the Black people you know did all of those things you said, that would be a very small sampling. He admitted after more discussion that he was no expert on this matter but was basing everything on what his parents had told him. We continued our discussion and when I left, I believe I had earned his respect. He could at least say that he had met one Black person who could not be stereotyped.

One of the things, like it or not, I was a trail blazer, a role model and I was under the microscope. That did not change for me in the corporate world. I have had to put a light on a lot of topics. But more importantly, I learned that: *"I must let my light so shine before men, that others might see my good works and glorify my Father which is in heaven."* **Amen.**

Words

By Aubrey B. Jones, Jr.

Sticks and stones can break people's
bones and your words can hurt them too.
So be careful what you say
and whom you say it to!

Your *tongue* is a ***mighty sword*** that ***can cut*** someone in two
So it is better to hold your tongue if you're not sure what to do
Your *tongue* is a ***powerful weapon*** that can cause some ***pain*** for you
So remember what you say can ***comeback*** to ***hurt*** you too!
You might not mean to use those words and to say them in that tone
But your ***ill-timed words*** are ***hurtful*** and cut through to the bone
You might say that you were joking and were just having some fun
But there is bleeding inside of a person because of what you have done

Sticks and stones can break people's
bones and your words can hurt them too.
So be careful what you say
and whom you say it to!

Your words can really hurt people although they might be true
So watch what you say and consider their feelings too
Your *words* can give you *power* but you don't have to be rude
So use this *power* in a *positive way* to improve your attitude
You can say that *"I'm sorry and I didn't mean to say that to you"*
But the damage is already done and there's something you need to do
You need to watch what you say and how you say it too
And always *think* before you say it - is a *wise* thing to do!

> Sticks and stones can break people's
> bones and your words can hurt them too.
> So be careful what you say
> and whom you say it to!

I'm Out of Here

After I graduated from UVA in 1963, I thought I would never return. I must admit that I was proud to be a graduate of UVA. In particular, I enjoyed the prestige and recognition of being one of the first Blacks to graduate from the university. I enjoyed the excitement of breaking the barriers of segregation. But I would not miss the stress and the pressures I endured for four and a half years. I liked being a part of a great tradition but I never really felt a part of the university. I felt like an unwanted guest at someone's home. So I was happy to leave because I had achieved my goal.

In 1987, I decided to attend the first weekend held by UVA's Black Alumni because they were honoring the Black Alumni of the 50s and 60s. Surprisingly, I had a great time. There were over 220 Black graduates in attendance. The keynote speaker was John Merchant, the first Black to graduate from the Law School. He challenged us to raise a half a million dollars for minority scholarships. This fund was named for **Walter N. Ridley**, the university's first Black graduate. As a result of this fund, the Black Alumni now have a reason to feel a part of UVA. Just as someone paved the way for us, we can continue to help the brothers and sisters who follow us. There are over 15,000 Black alumni in 2005.

I was invited back to UVA in 1990 to speak to the council of Black Student Leaders. They were concerned about a recent rash of racial incidents on the campus. Racial slurs were written on the sidewalks and some Whites displayed a hostile attitude toward some of the Black students. During my speech, I told them that I did not know how it was at UVA for them today but believed that it was much better than it was thirty years ago when I was there. I pointed out that they had a lot more support and activities. Also, I told them that I envied them for having

Black Student associations, fraternities, sororities, Office of African-American Affairs, Black professors and growing Black alumni. But I emphasized that I did not want to minimize any concerns that they had at that time.

My point was simply this: *"If we made it with much less support, then you can do it too!"* I told them I realized that many of the young brothers and sisters are unwilling to put up with the things we had to deal with thirty years earlier. And I agreed that they should not have to do so. But I reminded them that "life is full of obstacles and challenges and if they give up every time they are faced with challenges, they will never accomplish anything." Further, I stated that each of us has the power to do whatever we want to do. All we need to do is to keep the faith and believe in ourselves, and we can handle any challenge, including dealing with racism at UVA. I closed my speech with a poem I wrote entitled, *"You Can Do It Too!"* It was an upbeat tempo, rap-like poem that suggested six things that a student could do to get ahead in life. It was so well received by the students that I was inspired to write fifteen more poems in a rap-like style over a two-month period. These and other poems have been put to music and have been used successfully in the Philadelphia school system. The program is called *"I Can Do It Too! A Self-Esteem and Motivational Program for Young People."* Some of these poems, including *"You Can Do it Too!"* appear in this book.

You Can Do It Too!

By Aubrey B. Jones, Jr.

Listen everybody and you shall hear
About some facts of life that are really clear.

If you want to get ahead in life today
Then you better listen to what I'm about to say.
You can be anything you want to be
If you say to yourself it's up to me.
Let's listen to see what it takes.
Let's listen to see what it takes.

Now here's the first thing that you can do
And it's good for your friends and family too!
Be inquisitive — Ask questions.
Be inquisitive — Ask questions.

When you're in class and don't understand
Don't be afraid to raise your hand.
If you see a word that makes you query
Just look it up in the dictionary.
You're inquisitive — You ask questions.
You're inquisitive — You ask questions.

Here's the second thing you can do
And it's also good for me to do too.
Be smart — Don't follow the crowd.
Be smart — Don't follow the crowd.

When things around you are getting out of hand
Don't be afraid to take a stand.
If people around you are using dope
Then take your stand by just saying *"Nope."*

You're smart — You don't follow the crowd.
You're smart — You don't follow the crowd.

Here's a third thing that you can do
And others should consider this one too.
Think positive — It'll give you power.
Think positive — It'll give you power.

A positive attitude is really good
But that's hard to find in your neighborhood.
Thinking positive might seem outrageous
But a positive outlook is really contagious.
You think positive — You have the power.
You think positive — You have the power.

Here's the fourth thing for you to do
And I really love this one too.
Be confident — Say "Yes I can."
Be confident — Say "Yes I can."

You can be anything that you want to be
If you say to yourself it's up to me.
But you can do anything that you want to do
If you have the faith that it will happen to you.
You're confident — "Yes you are."
You're confident — "Yes you are."

Here's the fifth thing that you can do
And others must consider this one too.
Be diligent — Do your best.
Be diligent — Do your best.

It does not matter what you want to be
As long as you're the best that you can be.
There are no shortcuts to success today
So get ready to work hard for your pay.
You're diligent — You do your best.
You're diligent — You do your best.

Here's the sixth thing that you can do
And I am sure it will help others too.
Set goals — Know where you are going.
Set goals — Know where you are going.

When you decide on what you must do
Then write down your goals and keep them in view.
One goal or two, many or few — you make that call
But too many goals are almost as bad as no goals at all.
You set goals — You know where you are going.
You set goals — You know where you are going.

Here's the last thing I want to say
I hope that you have learned something today.
I know that at times things will get rough
And these will be the times for you to hang tough.
I know that you might just be a beginner
But don't give up because You can be a Winner!

Hang tough and never, never quit.
Hang tough and never, never quit.

—Because **You Can Do It Too!**

The Interview

UVA was a microcosm of what I was to face in the corporate world. It helped prepare me to deal with the challenges of being a minority in a predominately white corporate structure. During my third year, I had an interview with Philco Ford Corporation in the college placement office at UVA with a *Mr. H.R. Mann*. The only reason I signed up for the interview was to get some practice with my interviewing skills. To my surprise, the interview went extremely well and they invited me to call them when I was in my last year. During my last semester at UVA, I called *Mr. Mann* and told him that I was interested in working for Philco Ford. He told me someone would be in touch with me to set up a follow-up interview in Philadelphia. As he promised, I received a letter from a *Mr. Crass* who set up the interview for me.

I had never been to Philadelphia before and the company put me up at the Benjamin Franklin Hotel in downtown Philadelphia. My interview was in Fort Washington, Pa., a suburb of Philadelphia. I had to catch a local commuter train to get to the office. Once I got to the office, I told the receptionist that I had an appointment with *Mr. Crass*. When he came to the lobby, he looked right pass me as though I was not standing there. After a few minutes, I said, *"Mr. Crass"* and evidently he was surprised to see a Black man from UVA, applying for an engineering job. He was speechless for a moment and then he said, "Oh you're Mr. Jones." I said, "I believe you sent me a letter inviting me up for an interview?" He finally recovered from the shock of seeing me and asked me to wait in the lobby. After a few minutes, he gave me my itinerary for the day.

The rest of the interviews went well. When it was time for me to leave, *Mr. Crass* offered to take me to the train station so that I could go back to my hotel. But when we got to the train station, he dropped me off on the wrong side of the tracks and said to me, there is a gate you can go through and if it's locked you can *"climb over the fence."* He obviously was still uncomfortable dealing with me. After I looked at him like he was crazy, he said, "I'll drive you around to the other side." I told him to forget it and that I would rather walk. This might seem like an insignificant incident but it illustrates how some Whites were not ready to deal with a Black employee. I never saw *Mr. Crass* again but I did get a job offer that I accepted. Fortunately for me, *Mr. Crass **was not*** the hiring manager; he was in Human Resources.

Human Resource People typically do not have the authority to hire or fire someone from another department in a company. But they can influence the hiring. Although not in my case, they are usually the first to see you during the pre-screening interview. The person who visited UVA and interviewed me initially was not *Mr. Crass*. Therefore, it is important to watch what you say or do around people like *Mr. Crass* because they can be a roadblock to a real opportunity for you. The lesson here is don't let bigots like *Mr. Crass* keep you from getting to the real hiring manager.

GO FOR IT!

Aubrey B. Jones, Jr.

If it feels right for you
And it's something you really want to do
Go for it!

If it's a dream come true
And you don't know what to do
Go for it!

If it sounds good to you
And it's *legal* too
Go for it!

If it's believable to you
And it's achievable too
Go for it!

If there's someone in your way
Don't dismay
Go for it!

If there are obstacles in your way
Don't forget to pray
Go for it!

If your pride gets in the way
Don't let it lead you astray
Go for it!

You'll be happy that you did one day

IV. Life Philco-Ford's Plantation in the 1960s

How Does It Feel To Be Up North?

I was excited about receiving my first job offer and moving to Philadelphia, Pa. Philadelphia was an attractive location for me because it was far enough away from Richmond. Yet it was close enough for me to drive home to visit my family and friends when I wanted to do so. In my offer letter, they gave me the name of a Black man in personnel, Mr. *Smith*, who was suppose to help me find housing. I was assigned to work at Philco Ford's office located in Blue Bell, Pa., a suburb of Philadelphia. When I got in touch with Mr. *Smith*, he told me that he was having trouble finding a place close to Blue Bell. So he gave me two choices. I could either rent a room at a local motel or rent a room at the home of Mrs. Gladys Branch, a Black lady who lived in Penllyn, Pa. Since I had very little money, no car and no idea of what the community was like, I opted to live at Mrs. Branch's until I could afford to do better.

As quiet as it was kept, the reason Mr. *Smith* could not find a place for a young Black man in Blue Bell was because of discrimination. In Richmond, we knew where we could or could not live because there were signs that said, "White Only." But in Philadelphia and many other northern cities, some whites were more devious on how they discriminated. When a Black person tried to rent an apartment, they would tell you that there were no vacancies. As far as I was concerned, **the only difference between the south and parts of the north was geographical location.** Whites up north still had the same racist attitudes as those in the south but they did not want to admit that it was true. Whites used *segregation* in the south and *discrimination* in the north to *keep Blacks on the plantation.*

As it turned out, living in Penllyn was a blessing for me. It was a small Black community located a few miles outside of Philadelphia and very close to Blue Bell. Because most of the families had their roots in Virginia (Westmoreland County) they accepted me with open arms. I roomed at Mrs. Branch's home and I ate my meals at Mrs. Grace Wilson's house. Mrs. Wilson had a big family and she was a great cook. She would get insulted if you did not go back for seconds. I immediately felt like I was a part of a community with an extended family who made my transition from Richmond to Blue Bell very pleasant. Since I did not have or could afford a car, Mrs. Branch's daughter drove me to work and picked me up until I was able to make other arrangements.

I lived at Mrs. Branch's house for approximately five months. After many unsuccessful attempts of trying to find an affordable apartment in the Blue Bell and surrounding suburbs, I gave up. I did not want to take on another pioneering effort in looking for housing. To be honest, I did not want to live in an all White neighborhood. So I found an apartment in Philadelphia. There was discrimination in Philly but I had a lot more choices on where I could live. The downside of living in Philly was the city wage taxes and the public school system. The upside was there were lots of affordable housing in Philly and it was centrally located. This was important to me because there were many companies with opportunities within a reasonable commuting distance.

I Hate My Job

Working at Philco Ford as an engineer was a real learning experience. There were two other Black engineers in the Blue Bell Office: Leroy Green and Herb Morgan. Leroy was a retired captain from the army who had gone back to school after his discharge to get his engineering degree. He was much older than I and was married with several children. Herb was a quiet, smart young man who I never got to know too well because he stayed to himself. There was one woman, Connie Cottingham, who had a degree in math and was originally hired as the Librarian but after the library closed; she ended up being a secretary. Talk about being over-qualified!

I was working as a systems engineer in Philco Ford Communications Systems Division (CSD). At CSD our job was to design large microwave and tropo-scatter communications systems for the government. This meant that we had to write a lot of proposals to bid for the opportunities. If we won the contract, we would work with a number of subcontractors who actually designed and manufactured the equipment to meet Philco's specifications. I hated my first job because it was a "paper factory" where you wrote specifications, test procedures, reports and lots of proposals. I wanted some hands-on experience in designing circuits and equipment. I wanted to use some of the knowledge I had gained after spending four years in engineering school. Although this was not the original job that I had interviewed for, I accepted it. I thought that once I was hired I could easily move to another job if I did not like my assignment. Additionally, the money influenced me because the pay was very good.

So after several months of not liking what I was doing I made a rookie's mistake. I told my boss that I was unhappy with my work and that I would like to transfer to another department which could better utilize my skills. I truly thought it was the right thing to do. This was my first job and I did not have a mentor. I took it upon myself to "do the right thing." My boss just told me something like, "hang in there and give it a try." That was not what I wanted to hear but I did give it another try. When I did not get my first year review, I approached my boss to ask him why I had not been reviewed. He said that since I did not like my job he decided to delay my increase. What a rude awakening for me. How dare I complain to the slave master about my work? Once on the plantation, I was expected to do what I was told to do. No questions asked. I learned that it was not easy to change jobs on the plantation and that if I complained, there were consequences.

There was a manager, Phil Gonzales, who taught me about the facts of life in the corporate environment. He asked me if I would like to work in his group. His group was responsible for identifying and specifying test equipment for large systems. Not exactly what would have been my ideal job but I had a manager who had taken an interest in me and at least I could talk to him. I took advantage of this opportunity and turned a negative situation into something positive.

I developed a cataloging system to access the information which made it very easy to identify and justify test equipment. My system was a hit at the provisioning conference with the government, which was held in Colorado Springs. During the meeting, we had to justify every special tool and piece of test equipment needed to support the system. My quick access system allowed us to refer to each piece of equipment that was in question. Each item had a description and a justification on a single page so that it was easy to understand and justify. Today, this task would be much easier to do because we have access to personal computers.

Working in Phil's group helped get me back on track. I finally got my raise and a good performance review. Also, I got my first company paid trip to Colorado Springs. We had some free time so I was able to do some sight seeing and visit Pike's Peak. The lesson I learned is that you can learn something from most of your experiences in life. I learned how to make the best out of bad situations. I learned how to turn a negative situation into a positive one. But more importantly, I learned that you might not see the benefit of an experience immediately because it might take years for you to realize it. Later in life, I realized that all of my writing of proposals, specifications and reports helped me become a better writer. It taught me how to explain very complex things in simpler terms. This experience without a doubt helped me develop a writing style that allowed me to write ten books on programming computers in BASIC and Pascal.

Showcase Blacks

Most corporations in the 1960s advertised themselves as *equal opportunity employers*. But just because a company advertised itself as an *equal opportunity employer* did not necessarily mean that it was true. Nor did it mean that Black job hunters would readily flock to the company's personnel office. Many corporations complained that they could not find qualified Blacks. Because companies were under a lot of pressure from the Equal Employment Opportunity Commission (EEOC) to comply with the law, they had to show an effort. This was especially true for companies like Philco Ford whose primary customer was the federal government. One of the reasons some corporations could not hire more Blacks was because they only gave lip service to their effort. They said one thing but ended up doing something else. In short, these companies did not "walk the talk." Many Blacks who might have considered working in private industry flocked to the more secure government jobs because they did not trust some of the major corporations. They did not want to be used as *"the spook who set by the door"* or a *Showcase Black* who was on display when the government compliance inspectors came around.

At Philco Ford, they had a practice of using Black employees to help recruit other Blacks. Ostensibly it sounds like a good plan. But I did not want to be exploited. I did not want to be used as window dressing or for decoration. Nor did I want to be hired as an engineer and find myself assigned as the company's specialist in Black recruitment. I wanted an opportunity to work on challenging engineering projects. If a Black engineer is requested to go back to his alma mater to help recruit other engineers for his department, then that would probably be okay. But if they wanted me to go along to recruit Black accountants, secretaries, programmers or other administrative personnel, just because I was Black, I had a problem with that. So when I was approached by *Mr. H.R. Mann* of Personnel to help in recruitment of minorities, I refused. But after I refused, I wanted to make certain that he understood why I said "no."

So I wrote him a letter with some recommendations on how to go about recruiting more Blacks. Excerpts of the letter I sent to *Mr. Mann* follow this paragraph. I had only been employed by Philco Ford for two years at the time that I wrote the letter. It was pretty brazen of me to write this letter that included an unsolicited "Plans for Progress." But I felt that it was more important that he understood what I was saying. I did not want him to use our conversation as an excuse for not hiring more Blacks in the corporation. (Note the government used to have a program called *"Plans for Progress"* which each company was suppose to write a plan of action of how they were going to improve the hiring and promotion of minorities. Today it is called the *"Affirmative Action Plan."*)

(Excerpts of the letter to Mr. H.R. Mann)

I have given some thought to the conversation we had on Thursday, February 25, 1965. Basically, I believe that the recruitment of qualified Negroes for jobs is the responsibility of Personnel.

I was afraid that I might have left you with the wrong impression that I am a person who has lost concern for his people. I believe that every Negro who is in a position to do so should try to help in some way resolve the present problem of equal employment opportunities. The implementation of the solution to this problem depends on your relationship with the community. And therefore, since I am more familiar with the problem (from a Negro's perspective), I feel that I am in a better position to give you my perspectives of the problem and some recommended solutions.

These views are based on my experience and understanding of the company's policy together with a cursory survey of the opinions of fellow employees. The following is a break down of the major problem areas:

1. Hiring practices are dependent upon department manager's decisions which may or may not be consistent with Philco's policy of equal employment.
2. Present recruiting system needs an active equal employment opportunity manager.
3. Philco's image to the community does not readily attract qualified applicants.
4. Philco's image to the Negro Employees projects a certain amount of uncertainty and insecurity. That is, for example, how far can he advance in Philco? Will the management of Philco allow a Negro to advance in accordance with his capabilities and qualifications?

Recommendations

Although I realize that implementation of a practical program for equal employment opportunity is a difficult task, I believe that the following recommendations would be a step in the right direction.

1. A periodic review of the hiring practices of department managers should be made by Personnel to determine each manager's requirements for "qualified" people. That is, each department manager should define the term "qualified" which establishes his criteria for hiring. The person reviewing the practices does not necessarily have to be a minority but should be a person who is interested in establishing non-discriminatory practices. This periodic review would serve several purposes. For instance, Personnel could keep this information on file and during a preliminary interview could quickly determine whether or not to send an applicant to a certain department for an interview. In addition, if it was suspected that an applicant was not hired because of his race, it would be easy for management to detect a trend, and in turn, could remind the manager of Philco's non-discriminatory hiring practices.

2. I believe an active Equal Employment Manager should be hired who can help project a better image of Philco in the community. My concept of an active EEO manager is one who is also a public relations person who visits the community centers to encourage young people to continue school and make them aware of the opportunities with Philco and other industries in the area. This person should be in close contact with all the schools in the area and keep them abreast of the employment needs of Philco.

3. Philco should place "Help Wanted" advertisements in Black newspapers. Also Negroes should be used to advertise Philco's products.

4. Philco should set up some type of training program if they wanted to develop skills for potential new employees or upgrade the skills of existing employees.

5. If Philco accomplishes any of the above recommendations, I believe it will help destroy rumors among employees about a so-called "quota" Philco has on hiring Negroes. It would reflect a new positive image of truly being an Equal Opportunity Employer to its employees and to the community.

Conclusion
This Plan for Progress outlines certain positive and affirmative steps that should be taken by the Philco Ford Corporation. If implemented, it would encourage and help promote full equality of opportunity for qualified employees at all plants in every division of the company. It is recognized, however, that complete fulfillment of these non-discrimination policies and objectives is a long-range undertaking but in my opinion the above recommendations can be implemented now.

Who Helped You Write That Letter

Mr. Mann's reaction to my letter was cool at best. When I asked him about the letter, he said, **"It was a good letter by you or whomever you got to help you write it!"** I left it alone because I did not want to go there. I did not want to respond to his negative comment. But it was obvious to me by his comment that he did not think that I could have possibly written that letter by myself. I guess he thought I had someone from the NAACP to help me. The truth is that I wrote the letter and my wife typed it for me. It did take me some time and effort to compose the letter but I felt it would be worth it. I thought I was helping the company solve a problem. But I forgot that I was on the ***Philco Ford's corporate plantation*** and I was supposed to do what I had been told to do. Nobody asked me nor did they care about what I thought. But I was one of those "smart a..." Negroes trying to make trouble for White folks. I was one of those Showcase Blacks who forgot that he was not supposed to think or be creative. I was a troublemaker and must be dealt with.

Interestingly, some of the recommendations that I made in that letter were used by a number of companies a few years later. Most of the things I recommended are common practices in corporations today. But the problem with Philco at the time was that the Black community perceived it as a racist company. And with other options available to the skilled and professional Blacks, they did not want to or need to come to Philco for a job.

As I recall, nothing ever happened as a result of my letter. One of the things that I learned is that if you take on the system you had better "walk the chalk line." I always made certain that I took care of business first. My work record was above reproach and it would be difficult for anyone to cite me for not doing my job.

OEO Plant Visit

For companies like Philco that had government contracts, there was an annual visit by a representative from the Office of Employment Opportunities (OEO). Many Blacks including myself were annoyed by the way they conducted their plant tours. I was so annoyed that I wrote a letter to Personnel complaining about the visit. In November 1965, the OEO representative and several people from Personnel were walking through the office making a "head count" of Blacks. When he spotted me sitting at my desk, he walked over and introduced himself as Mr. *Knox*. I was the only Black of over 25 other engineers located in a large office that had no partitions.

When Mr. *Knox* approached me, I was talking to my supervisor. He began asking questions like: "How are you being treated here?" and "Are you permitted to attend meetings and conferences like all of the other engineers?" I was so embarrassed because I was put on the spot in front of my boss and others. I thought that the questions were ridiculous and that Mr. *Knox* did not have a clue as to what he should be looking for. Most companies who had government contracts openly treated their employees fairly.

My biggest complaint was that this conversation should have been in private. The way the interview was handled could have aroused resentment of my coworkers. Although I was not having any problems at the time, some of my coworkers could have thought that I was receiving some type of special treatment or that I had brought some kind of complaint against them. So I wrote a letter to personnel to complain about the practice. A copy of this letter is included.

(Copy of Letter on OEO Visit)

To: H.R. Mann
From: A. Jones
Date: 11-11-1965

Subject: Visit of OEO Representative

This letter serves to inform you on how the visit by Mr. Knox, of the Office of Equal Opportunities, affected me. First of all, I was somewhat embarrassed at being called from a conference with my supervisor to meet Mr. Knox and to talk with him in the presence of my coworkers. I feel this is not the way it should have been done.

If a representative from this organization wants to talk with an employee, he should do it privately. The manner in which the discussion was carried out tends to put an employee "on the spot." For example, it might appear that a minority employee is receiving some special treatment or that he is unsatisfied with the conditions of his working environment. It also might appear that the minority has registered a complaint with the government or some other agency. These are only a couple of the reasons why it should not have been done; however, I feel these are the most important of a large number.

As far as I am concerned, this defeats the purpose of the visit. By that I mean, to single out an employee because he is a minority only reminds his coworkers of his presence. In most cases, after a minority has been on the job for some time his presence is usually unnoticed as such to most of his coworkers as far as employee work relations are concerned.

I realize that it is the prerogative of an OEO representative to talk with an employee "on the spot." However, I feel if the OEO representative knew the effect this has on a minority and his coworkers, he would refrain from this practice. In fact, I feel that Philco should pass on this information to Mr. Knox. I am certain that he would appreciate it.

Finally, I realize that you stated initially that Mr. Knox did not want to disturb me or anyone else, but you wanted him to meet me because of a letter I had written to you per our discussion some time ago. However, I would like to remind *you that in 1964 while at Plant 37, Mr. Traub of the same organization, approached me in a similar manner. In fact, he stopped at my desk and began to ask me questions; it was upon my request that we later moved to the cafeteria where we continued our conversation in private.*

An equal employment opportunity in industry is still in its infancy. Although both government and industry are making efforts to promote equal employment opportunities, no one knows all the answers to the problems. I feel that everyone has to play his part in obtaining this common goal of equal employment. Therefore I feel I am doing my part by submitting recommendations or suggestions such as in this letter. I hope you accept it in the spirit that it is given.

Did it Do Any Good?

Since this was not the first time that an OEO representative embarrassed me, I decided to write a letter to *H.R. Mann* in Personnel. This letter illustrates how I continued to make suggestions when I felt it was necessary. After a visit a year earlier by an OEO representative, my wife was hired as a secretary. This happened because I told the representative that there were not any problems for engineers in Philco. But if he looked around he would have noticed that there were no minority clerks or secretaries in the plant. He told me that the reason given by Philco was that Blacks could not travel to the plants because they were in the suburbs. I told him that my wife was an experienced secretary but could not find a job in Philadelphia. He wanted to know if she had applied for a job at Philco. I told him she already had several interviews with Personnel but to no avail. On the very next day, I received a call from personnel who said; "Mr. Jones I understand your wife is looking for a job. Please ask her to give me a call." I said, "Thank you very much." She was hired.

Most Blacks felt that the OEO visits were a waste of time. It is very difficult for an outsider to determine the conditions of a company by a mere visit. He can count the heads but he won't get an honest feedback. I must admit that I was surprised how fast my wife was hired. But she could have been hired long before that visit by the OEO. So I guess the visit did some good after all. I am certain my letter did not stop the annual visits but no one from OEO ever approached me again.

The Interview at IBM's Plantation

Marketing and Sales jobs have always been the glamour jobs in the industry. In the 1960s and even today, there is a belief by some that a Black salesperson cannot compete successfully against Whites. The belief was that successful selling requires building a relationship with a customer, and therefore, this would work against Blacks. That is, many believed that White customers would not buy from a Black salesperson. Unfortunately, that was true of some Whites and probably still is somewhat true today. Because of this, it was very difficult for Blacks to break into a sales position. IBM and Xerox were two companies that had a good reputation of offering equal opportunities to Blacks. So when I heard of an opportunity for a Systems Engineer with IBM in the Philadelphia Sales Office, I applied for the job. What I learned was that just because a company advertises as an Equal Opportunity Employer it did not necessarily mean that everyone who worked for that company bought into the program.

When I went to the IBM office, I was greeted warmly by the secretary but things went downhill after that. I was so upset about what happened I wrote a letter to the President and CEO, Mr. Thomas J. Watson, Jr. The letter speaks for itself so I have included a copy.

(Copy of the Letter to T. J. Watson, Jr)

6303 Morton Street
Philadelphia, Pa 19144
July 8, 1967

Mr. Thomas J. Watson, Jr.
President
IBM Corporation
Old Orchard Road
Armonk, New York 10504

Dear Mr. Watson:

Knowing that IBM is interested in the image it projects to the public, I feel certain that you would be interested in an incident that occurred during an interview at your Philadelphia office. I was somewhat hesitant about writing this letter. But after discussing the incident with several friends, who are employed by IBM, I was persuaded to write you a letter. They assured me that IBM's policy on Equal Opportunity is a fact.

I applied for a position as a system's engineer with IBM's Marketing Department. I was interviewed by a Mr. Jim Crow*, Manager of Account Marketing, at the Philadelphia office on April 28, 1967. The results of the interview were very humiliating and embarrassing for me. I will attempt to describe the interview in the following paragraphs.

First of all, my interviewer had not read my resume before he interviewed me. In fact, he did not remember that I had submitted a resume although I received a letter from him *prior to the interview notifying me that he had received it. I reminded him that I had submitted a resume. Then, apologetically, he began looking for my resume and eventually his secretary found it.*

During the interview, little was asked of me about my technical capabilities. We discussed current events and the social problems of the Negro. Being a Negro, a discussion of racial problems with Whites was not new to me. He emphasized to me that he was Irish and that the Irish had similar problems as Negroes a long time ago. I told him that I was aware of such problems but if he had not mentioned to me that he was Irish I would not have known it. I pointed out to him that it is easier to discriminate against people who are easily identified, such as the Negro, and that his analogy was neither applicable nor appropriate. He had no comment on this statement.

After over an hour of this type of discussion, he said to me, "Are you conscious of your diction?" I told him "Yes." He informed me that there were several words that I did not pronounce correctly and his reason for telling me this was that he was trying to help me. I told him that I was conscious of these words. I told him that when I speak rapidly I do not enunciate all of the phonetics in certain words. I explained to him that this was partly do to my southern vernacular. After this criticism, I was really upset although I tried not to show it. I know that my diction is not so poor that it distracts from my conversation because both my former and present jobs required talking with the customer, my manager and other employees without any complaints so far. Further I did not go to IBM to seek "Help" but to seek employment. I felt that IBM might be interested in my technical background and experience.

Mr. Crow also said: "You look like a young man who wants to get ahead so that's why I am telling you these things." He did not realize that I have already come a long way relative to my background and if I did not want to get ahead, I would have been content to stay in the poverty I knew as a child. I can not explain fully the impact that such statements had on me. I feel that if I have some characteristics that are not acceptable to IBM's standards then I should not be hired but I should not have to be subjected to such criticisms during an interview.

Finally, I was asked to take an aptitude test. This surprised me because I did not think a person with my experience required testing. I informed him that I only had a half day off from my job and also that I was not in the proper mood to take a test. He insisted that I take the test and said it was simple and short. So I took the test during the lunch period. I could not concentrate on the test because all of my self-confidence was temporarily destroyed and I was very upset. In fact, all I wanted to do was to get out of that office as fast as I could. As a result, I did not do well on the test, and was told that, based on the test results, I was not considered for employment.

My purpose for writing this letter is not to seek employment but to help prevent future applicants from being subjected to similar embarrassment and humiliation.

Sincerely yours,

Aubrey B. Jones Jr.

Aftermath of the IBM Interview

Upon receiving my letter, Mr. Watson called for a detailed investigation of the incident. I received a telephone call from IBM's District Manager to meet with him on July 19 in his office to discuss my interview. During the meeting, I could not prove racial discrimination because everything the interviewer said was very ambiguous. In fact, the District Manager said that *Mr. Crow* did not really mean what he said to me because he was just "joshing!"

Recognizing that the District Manager was trying to defend the actions of *Jim Crow*, I told him that I did not come there to debate the issues but to clarify any questions that he might have about what happened. My sole purpose was to make certain that no one else had to go through what I encountered during an interview. I truly believe it was racially motivated but I could not prove it. It is always tough to prove unless it's blatant. So I got the District Manager to admit that the interview was handled in an "Unprofessional manner." A lesser charge which he and the company accepted.

After the interview, I received a letter from the district manager thanking me for coming in to discuss my concerns with him. He said, *"It is unfortunate that your interview caused you the concern that it obviously did and I can assure you that we are taking steps to improve the procedure in the future. As we discussed today, we would be happy to talk to you again about IBM should you feel so disposed?"* I would not even think of going to IBM after that incident so I turned down his offer.

But the highlight of this incident was receiving a letter of apology from the President of IBM on his personal stationary. I still have this letter from Mr. Watson which read as follows:

(Copy of the Letter from T. J Watson, Jr.)

Thomas J Watson Jr.
Old Orchard Road
Armonk, New York 10504

6303 Morton Street
Philadelphia, Pa. 19144
August 7, 1967

"Dear Mr. Jones,

Thank you for your recent letter about your employment interview.
I have reviewed the investigation that followed and regretfully concluded that you were treated inconsiderately and insensitively. I deeply regret the imposition on you, and I appreciate your writing me.

Best wishes.

Sincerely yours,

Signed (T. J Watson)"

On the plantation, it's okay for the slave master to talk down to you. But I made the mistake up standing up to him so he had to put me in my place. I came with good credentials and was dressed appropriately in my dark blue three-piece suit with a white shirt. But he had to let me know that no matter how smart I thought I was, I was not at his level. He tried to whip me mentally, he tried to kill my spirit, and he tried to keep me on the plantation.

I do not know if my letter helped any minorities who applied for a position with IBM afterwards. But I feel that my letter did make a difference. I felt that I had to take a stand, and in this case, I had nothing to lose and a lot to gain-**RESPECT!** The lessons learned from this letter and others that I wrote over my career are: *1) To thine on self be true! 2) To start at the top* and *3) "That the pen is mightier than the sword!"*

To thine own self be true!
"This above all: to thine ownself be true,
And it must follow, as the night the day,
Thou canst not then be false to any man."
-Shakespeare-Hamlet

"Unless we can be true to ourselves, we cannot be true to others. Those of us that gave our life to another at the cost of losing who we are in the process will have a hard time being true to ourselves."
Courtesy of LanThi and Dr. Irene Matiatos, Copyright© 2000.

Gaining Respect on the Plantation

Here is one of the things that I recognized very early about working in the corporate environment. Many people formed their opinions of me without even knowing me. Blacks are discriminated against by some Whites who have made up their minds beforehand that "we are all in the same bag." My experiences in the Air Force and UVA prepared me to deal with people who would not like me although I had not done anything to them. My survival strategy was simple: *Accept the fact that people might not like me but that it was more important that they respect me.* I felt that over time when they learned more about my work ethics, my integrity and my intellect they still might not like me but they would learn to respect me. And over time my strategy did work.

Lack of respect by some White coworkers is sometimes so subtle that they do not even recognize that what they are doing is being disrespectful to you. These situations can create barriers on the job especially if it is not "nipped in the bud." One situation that created barriers on the job was the practice of a White coworker telling ethnic jokes. I realize that jokes are told about Jews, Italians and Polish people as well as Blacks. But ethnic jokes can get out of hand. How do you turn it off once it gets going? If you laugh at a joke about an Italian, what are you going to do if you hear a derogatory joke about Blacks? As a Black man who was trying to establish a level of respect from my peers, I would not tolerate the telling of ethnic jokes to me. Especially offensive to me were the jokes where the Black person was using poor English like "I is" and "I wants." And some Whites were so brazen that they would even try to get away using the "N" word.

I did not have to be nor wanted to be reminded that some of my brothers and sisters were uneducated due to circumstances beyond their control. And if a White coworker came to me in private to tell me a derogatory joke about a Jew, my first thought was "what is he saying about Blacks behind my back?" Therefore, I adopted the position that I would not participate in telling jokes with anyone regardless of what ethnic group the joke was about. For example, one day one of my White coworkers approached me saying: "Aubrey you seem like an opened -minded person let me tell you — —-" and before he could get it out, I said, "I don't want to hear any ethnic jokes!" He apologized immediately and backed off. The next time someone tried to tell a joke around me, this person interrupted and said, "Aubrey doesn't like ethnic jokes." He got the message and maybe I gained a little bit of Respect.

During the 1960s, many Black professionals complained

about the "unofficial tests" on the job. This was true especially if you were new on a job. Here is how it worked. A White coworker would approach you with a problem to which he already knew the answer. The unsuspecting Black did not usually catch on at first but it did not take long for you to find out what was really going down. I asked one on my coworkers one time, "Why are you asking me this question, you obviously know the answer to it? Are you testing me?" My coworker's response was, "I am not testing you; I just wanted to know what your capabilities are?" He was not my supervisor so why should he have been concerned about my capabilities. Most whites would not admit that they were "testing" you if confronted. But it did happen and it continued until the coworker was satisfied that you were a capable person or until you got fed up with it and put a stop to it. Jackie Robinson was one of my heroes. I knew what he had to go through to break into baseball. I knew he had to put up with a lot of negative and racially motivated stuff. I am not trying to imply that what I went through was even close to what Jackie Robinson had to endure. But whenever you are the first, you have to put up with a lot. Jackie Robinson earned the respect of everyone in baseball even some of the people who did not even like him. He set the standard for me and other Blacks who wanted to earn the respect of peers.

"In life you might have to work for and with people who don't like you!"

"It's more important that people respect you."

"Be more concerned with your character than your reputation, because your character is what you really are,
while your reputation is merely what others think you are."

Respect

by Aubrey B. Jones, Jr

        I know that everybody won't like me
        But it's more important that they respect me
        Respect myself is the first thing I should do
        And then others might respect me too
        Respect is something that I might receive if I ask
        But earning respect is no easy task
        Respect is something that I must earn
        And it is also something that I can learn
        Respect is **not** built on what the eyes can see
        But respect is built on what's inside of me

Some people judge me by what they see
Instead of trying to learn more about me
Some people might not like the color of my skin
But they can learn to respect my values within
Some people might praise my athletic ability
But I prefer that they respect my mental facility
Some people might like me for my good looks
But they will respect me more when I hit the books
Some people might like me for the way that I dress
But they will respect me more when I am a success
Respect is *not* built on what the eyes can see
But respect is built on what's inside of me

        I know that everybody won't like me
        But it's more important that they respect me
        Respect myself is the first thing I should do
        And then others might respect me too
        Respect is something that I might receive if I ask
        But earning respect is no easy task
        Respect is something that I must earn
        And it is also something that I can learn
        Respect is **not** built on what the eyes can see
        But respect is built on what's inside of me

V. The HNIC on Control Data's Plantation

My Transition from an Engineer to a Manager

While at Philco Ford, I was interviewed by Univac and offered a position as a project engineer. After I was unable to gain experience in circuit design at Philco Ford, I decided to make the best out of my situation and developed my expertise in systems engineering. This move helped me get the job at Univac. I left Philco because they were running out of meaningful work for me to do. Engineers were being laid off and there were no major contracts on the horizon. The last major contract, the AUTODIN Store and Forward Message Switching System, provided me the opportunity to get some hands on experience in the design and testing of a major system. The unique aspect about this project was the pilot system was on site at Philco. Our responsibility was to make certain that the system met all of the specifications so that the government would approve it and accept the system.

At Univac, I worked in a lab which was responsible for circuit and equipment design, something I wanted to do three years earlier. But I was hired because of my knowledge of large communications systems. I enjoyed working in the lab at Univac. At the time, I was working with some of the brightest people in the communications field. This was also a fun-loving group nicknamed "F-Troop" after a popular TV show. My manager, Jerry Randle, a little unorthodox in his management style, but he was a regular guy when dealing with people. He did not care what color you were as long as you got the job done. But despite my pleasant experience in this Lab, I had to leave when the company decided to move all of its communications operations to Salt Lake City Utah. I felt that Salt Lake City, a Mormon city, would not be a great place for a Black family to live. So I left Univac after approximately eighteen months to go to work for Control Data Corporation (CDC).

In 1967, I was offered a position as Product Manager at CDC's Valley Forge Division. CDC was a very progressive company. It was growing so fast that it had to look outside of the corporation for managers. It gave me a great opportunity to try out management. I gave myself two years to try it and if I did not like it, I would go back to engineering. Product Management was a good transitional job for me because it required a thorough understanding of the products, the competition and the market. It also required that I stay somewhat technical because I had to understand the features, functions and other requirements of my products.

I reported to *Bill Ivy*, a Cornell University Engineering graduate with an MBA. He was a very conservative Ivy Leaguer. The thing I remember most about Bill was that it took him a long time to make a decision. He would always ask for more data or more details. This is a classic way to delay making a decision. As frustrating as it was for me at times to get *Bill* to make a decision, I got along well with him otherwise. He was a man of high integrity and seemed to generally care about people. I was hired as the Product Manager for Punched Card Equipment and my counterpart, *Larry Bravado*, was the Product Manager for Magnetic Tape Equipment. We manufactured both

Card and Tape equipment at the facility. As the product manager, I had a lot of responsibility but very little real authority. My authority was based on the knowledge by others that when I made a request; I had the support of the general manger of the division. Since everyone in the division knew that I had his support, I used it as clout when it was necessary.

The first two years at CDC were exciting for me and I learned a lot. There were many challenges but I gave it my best shot. I did whatever it took to get me up to speed. My experience at CDC was the foundation for my career in management. I had the opportunity to work with some of the best managers in the industry. CDC's top management team headed by Bill Norris was known to be innovative and sharp.

My Unique Role at CDC

When I was hired, I was the only Black manager at the Valley Forge Plant. Many Black employees sought me out for advice or direction because they did not feel comfortable talking to their White supervisors. I became the unofficial ombudsman for the Black employees. I listened to their concerns and complaints then determined if they were substantial enough to bring it to management's attention. One of the things that was established very quickly was that if I came to Personnel with an issue it was usually valid. By default, I became the HNIC or "Head Negro in Charge" as the Black employees "jokingly" called me. It is analogous to the "straw boss" on the plantation or the Black slave driver who was assigned the task of keeping the other slaves in line. But the major difference was I was not afraid to confront my White slave masters on this plantation.

A young White woman applied for a job on the assembly line at CDC. Her husband, who was Black, also worked there. When she came in for an interview, the interviewer asked her why she wanted to leave her present job as a telephone operator to work on the assembly line. She told him that she wanted to spend more time with her family and that she could not do that now because she worked on the night shift. After some additional discussions, the interviewer told her that she was *over-qualified* for the job. He told her because she worked in an office environment that she would not be able to adjust to an assembly line job. She pleaded with him to give her an opportunity and that she was confident that she would be okay. I need to point out that these assembly line jobs were usually filled by housewives who had no experience and, in many cases, who just worked for short periods of time to pick up some extra money. In addition, the facility was very clean and modern which made the working environment acceptable to most people. The young interracial couple felt that they were being discriminated against. So her husband approached me and asked for help.

After he explained the situation to me, I met with the interviewer. I told him that the couple felt that they were being discriminated against because they were an interracial couple. Surprisingly, he admitted that he did it to protect them. "I did it to save them from unnecessary pressures from other employees." He justified his decision based on his experience of hiring a White woman married to a Black man. He pointed out that because the White female employee was harassed and ostracized by her coworkers, she resigned. I told him that although his intentions might have been good, his actions were against company policy. The interviewer maintained that he was only trying to protect the woman, her husband, and the company from a potential problem. He admitted that he really did not know what to do so he took the easiest way out. He was afraid to tell her the real reason because he thought that she would not understand, and that would have caused a problem for the company. I suggested that he tell her his concerns and let her decide on what she wanted to do.

I asked the employee had he considered the possible consequences if his wife was hired? He said, "To tell you the truth I never really thought about it." So I suggested that he talk it over with his wife first and let me know his decision. Before he even left my office, he told me he was certain that a hostile environment would not upset his wife because she really knew how to handle herself. So he agreed to talk it over with her. On the next day, he told me that she was still interested in the job and requested another interview. She got the interview and was hired. She started work without incident and remained on the job for some time thereafter. It was not my job to step in and try to solve a personnel problem in a department where I had no jurisdiction. But as the only Black manager in the office, the employee felt comfortable to come to me with his problem. And I felt obligated to help.

Sometimes, I can't believe some of the things Whites tried to get away with in the 1960s and 1970s, although I was there to see it and hear it for myself. Here is another example of how the same personnel representative insulted the intelligence of two Black women and thought he could get away with it. Two Black women applied to CDC for a job as assembly line workers. One of the applicants had a car and planned to provide transportation for her friend. The interviewer told the woman with the car that he would be in touch with her after he checked her references. He told the other woman that she would have to wait and see *if her friend liked the job* before he would hire her. Supposedly, his concern was if the driver did not like the job, he would lose two people at the same time due to a lack of transportation.

I became involved when an employee, who was a friend of the two women, approached me and asked for some help. I agreed to help and learned that the interviewer said that he was using this approach to see if the woman had any initiative because if she could find a back-up ride he would know that she really wanted to work. I resolved the issue by providing the interviewer with a list of names of employees who said that they would be happy to provide transportation if needed. This recruiter was either naive or biased but in either case, because of his poor judgment damaged the image of the company. Most of the Black employees were convinced that the interviewer actions were racially motivated. As a Black manager, the Black employees expected me to get involved. Personnel on the other hand was getting a little annoyed at me putting them on the spot. What they did not know was that for every problem I brought to them that there were three or four that they never heard about. I continued to play this role until they finally hired a Black in personnel who could handle many of these issues.

I cannot speak for other Black managers but I felt an obligation to stand up against the system when I knew I was in a position to make a difference. I have been criticized by some of my managers in the past. Onetime at CDC, my boss called me in to complain that *"I had been seen spending too much time with the Black employees."* What he was referring to in particular was that I would eat lunch most of the time with the Black employees. My attitude then was my lunchtime was my time to do whatever I wanted to do. I used that time to "cool out" for a few minutes from a hectic day. I did not want to talk shop on my lunch break. Hindsight is 20-20 as they say. Perhaps, I should have spent more time going out to lunch with the other managers. I know I gave the impression that I did not want to be bothered with them. But I knew that some of the managers preferred not to socialize with me and I never pushed myself on anyone. It's hard to compare the corporate environment today with what it was like forty years ago. But if you are going to get ahead in the corporations today you have to spend some time socializing with your peers, like it or not. It was probably one of the reasons

I did not advance further in the corporations. But I took pride on being independent and not kissing up to anyone to get ahead. And I still won't do that today.

The Last Straw

I used to believe that all you had to do was to work hard and you would be rewarded accordingly. Perhaps this is true when you are an individual contributor but it is definitely not true when you are in management. Once I was speaking at a college and a student asked me how I would evaluate my performance on the job. I told him that I gave myself "A+" on performance on the job and an "F" on company politics. I have never been good at playing company politics although I have gotten a little better at it. Until I really learned how to play the game, I suffered. I was passed over for a number of promotions without explanation during my career. But the last straw for me was when someone I hired and helped train was promoted over me and became my boss.

This was the ultimate blow. *"The last straw!"* I have always believed that "the pen is mightier than the sword." So I wrote one of my infamous letters to the president of CDC, Mr. Norris. He had a reputation of being a straight shooter and he was very involved in helping to improve the socio-economic condition of minorities. He was instrumental in opening up manufacturing facilities in the inner cities of Washington D.C. and Minneapolis. He also opened up facilities on an Indian reservation. When I was passed over at CDC without explanation, I decided to ask Mr. Norris for help. The following letter is very detailed and really tells the story.

(Copy of the letter to Mr. Norris)

9999 E. Sedgwick St.
Philadelphia, Pa. 19150
November 7, 1970

Mr. W. C. Norris
President
Control Data Corporation
Minneapolis, Minnesota 55440

Dear Mr. Norris:

When I accepted a position with CDC as Product Manager over three years ago, I thought that I had found a "home." I saw an opportunity to work with a company that was not only concerned with the problems of business but also concerned with the socio-economic problems of the nation. I have always been impressed with caliber of CDC's management team and I was also very proud to be a part of that team until now. The reason I am writing to you is because maybe you can help restore my faith in CDC's management.

To be more specific, I would appreciate if you can provide an answer to the following questions for me.

1. How can you justify promoting an individual from a **supervisor** to **director** when other more qualified people are available?

2. Why is it that of the three director's positions open at Valley Forge in the last six months in areas of my experience and background, I was not considered for any of the positions although it was felt by many including myself, that I was qualified to hold these positions?

3. What happened to the practice of promoting from within? I have seen several individuals leave CDC who were here when I started and returned later for higher level positions.

These are but three of the many questions I would like answered. However, before you answer these questions, there is one situation I would like to bring to your attention in more detail because I need a logical explanation from someone. The one situation is as follows.

A little over a year after I was hired, we hired a product specialist who came to us from the shipbuilding industry. This individual had a degree in Business Administration but knew nothing about the computer industry. Normally in Product Management, we try to hire people with both a technical and a business background although it is a tough combination to find. After the product specialist started to work, he was concerned about his opportunity for advancement. He stopped by my office for some advice on what I thought his opportunities were in Product Management. He was concerned that his opportunity for advancement might be limited because he did not have a technical background. I told him that there were several positions in Product Management which did not really require a technical background. I also told him not to be concerned over this fact and assured him that he could pick up most of the technical terminology required for the position through on-the-job-training. I also offered my assistance to help bring him on board in any way that I could.

This product specialist, *Jim Brash,* * remained in this position for over a year. When the department expanded, he was promoted to Supervisor of Scheduling and

Forecasting. At that time, Card and Tape products were in one division and our department basically consisted of a Director, two Product Managers and two Supervisors. When the decision was made to split the division into Card Products and Tape Products. My boss, *Bill Ivy,* * was assigned as Director of Product Management in the Tape Products Division. I was assigned as Manager of Product Management for the Card Products Division reporting to *Bob Petersburg.* * After only six months in his position, *Mr. Brash,* (who was concerned about his future) was promoted to Director of Master Scheduling and Facilities Planning on *Colonel Kickbutt's* * staff.

When this organization was announced, I was very disappointed and demoralized. I approached my former boss, *Bill Ivy,* and asked him why did this happen. He told me that he had nothing to do with the decision and that *Mr. Brash* certainly would not have been his recommendation. He suggested that I talk with *Colonel Kickbutt* since it was his unilateral decision.

So I met with the colonel to ask him to explain why he chose Mr. *Brash* over me. I pointed out that I was very disappointed and hurt by his appointment. I also asked him to tell me what I had done wrong, if anything, so that I would prepare myself for the next opportunity. *Colonel Kickbutt* assured me that he was satisfied with my performance and that the new Director's position was entirely different from the Product Management function. He said that the position was for "Master Scheduling and Facilities Planning only" and that I would be responsible for all of the Product Management functions.

As it turned out, the Director of Master Scheduling started involving himself in Product Management functions. I complained to my new boss, *Bob Petersburg,* * and explained to him that we did not have a workable situation. I told him that there were too many people in the division with the same functions. I was assured that this would change and that I would be responsible for all Product Management functions. However, this situation continued to deteriorate.

On Wednesday November 4, 1970, I was called into *Bob Petersburg's* office and told that there would be a reorganization and that Product Management departments would be combined under the direction of the former Supervisor of Product Management, (*Mr. Brash*). He could not give me any more details. He said that this was *Colonel Kickbutt's* decision and that he did not have a chance to discuss it with him.

Mr. *Brash* is a bright, young aggressive individual. But he cannot come close to matching my experience, background and overall ability. Consequently, I do not feel he is ready to handle the responsibility of Product Management. There are many people at Valley Forge including other managers and directors who "privately" agree with me on this point. When the word leaked out about the pending reorganization, some of the people in my group became very upset and indicated that they would like to start some type of protest. I told them that I appreciated their support but this was my problem and not to get involved. *Colonel Kickbutt* probably has a good reason for doing what he did but there is still the question- "Why?" Although Mr. *Brash* is bright, it will be difficult for me to work under his direction, when I feel that he is not qualified for this position. He has not been exposed to many of the aspects of the Product Management Function. I cannot be motivated by someone I will have to train to handle his position.

I asked other managers and directors at Valley Forge who knew about the situation to give me a logical explanation. No one can. But everyone has his own version on why it happened. I ask you the question, Mr. Norris; "Why did it happen?" I had partially recovered from the fact that Mr. *Brash* was promoted from supervisor to director after I was assured that his position would not overlap with mine. But to accept him as my boss, Mr. Norris is the "Coup de grace!"

I did not tell you initially that I was Black because I wanted you to look at the situation without respect to the color of the individuals involved. I am a very open-minded person and I never like to make a serious charge of racial discrimination unless I have eliminated all other possibilities. I have not had any major problems in CDC because of my race. I am still looking for a logical explanation on why after three years I am still a product manager. Yet people are brought in from the outside as directors or even worse, people who were in the company when I started, left the company and returned as directors.

Mr. Norris, I am becoming suspicious that I have now become a "Showcase Black." That is, the one Black in middle management that is available when the Office of Equal Opportunity representative comes around for a "head count." I hope that I am wrong. I would rather my boss to tell me that my work does not meet his expected performance level. However, this would be very difficult to do that after three years in the same position with good performance reviews.

I apologize for writing such a long letter but I felt that it was necessary to give all the details from my point of view.

I realize that writing this letter will jeopardize my career with CDC but this does not concern me. My only concern is that I will be able to prevent others from encountering the same type of frustration and disappointment I have encountered.

Sincerely Yours,

Aubrey B. Jones Jr.

*Mr. *Brash* and other names in italics are not the real names here although I did use his real name in the original letter.

Lessons Learned

After I sent the letter to Mr. Norris, I met with *Colonel Kickbutt* again. This time he told me the reason he promoted *Mr. Brash* over me was that *Mr. Brash* was much more aggressive than I was in solving problems. I said to him, if you are telling me that you want someone to jump when you say jump and not to think or question the reason why, then you picked the right person for that job. I am not interested in any position where I am not allowed to think and use my knowledge to help solve a problem.

This was my first Management job and I was very naive about company politics. I did not realize that qualifications do not necessarily play a role in promotions. If you want to promote someone to your staff, you do it. I learned also that people will not be honest with you. Although it was *Colonel Kickbutt's* decision, the management team knew what was going on but they did not want to get involved. I also learned that people promote those people they like. They like those people who have the right chemistry or, in some cases, people who will cater to their every need. I learned that my laid back style gave the appearance that I was not an aggressive individual or too conservative in my approach.

Colonel Kickbutt was a very interesting person. When I was hired, he was the General Manager of the Division. He was a retired army officer and an active alumnus of Ohio State University. His military background carried over into his corporate position. Most of his staff were afraid of him. He had the ability to chew you out and make you feel like hell. But after he chewed you out, he could talk to you like nothing ever happened. It was not a personal thing with him when he chewed you out. It was all business and his autocratic style of management. I must admit that I learned a lot by observing *Colonel Kickbutt* in action. I had the opportunity to sit in meetings and silently make decisions without him knowing it. I would make the decisions in my mind. But I had the luxury to wait to see if I would have made the right decision when the effect of the decision was finally known. It was a kind of live case study for me, which helped me learn about management's decision-making process.

I did not leave CDC immediately because I did not want to leave on a bad note. So I stayed with CDC another year and was responsible for the division winning a major design contract. I was the project/proposal manager for our bid to win the Washington Area Metropolitan Transportation Authority Automatic Fare Collection System. We won the contract although no one gave CDC a chance in the beginning. After we won the contract, my "stock" went up in the corporation. Everyone was congratulating me on the great job we had done.

Now, it was time to leave. To *Colonel Kickbutt's* credit, he called me in his office after I turned in my resignation. He said to me "Aubrey, I made some assumptions about you earlier and I was wrong. I just wanted you to know that." I really appreciated *Colonel Kickbutt* telling me that because he didn't have to do it especially since I was leaving. It was never personal with him and it takes a big man to say, "I was Wrong!" I still have a lot of respect for *Colonel Kickbutt*. He taught me a lot.

Thank You Very Much!
by Aubrey B. Jones, Jr.

Here's what you need to do when someone criticizes you:

"Thank you very much for that today!"
"Is there anything else you'd like to say?"

No one likes to be criticized
Whether you are right, wrong or otherwise
Handling criticism might not be easy to do
Because it might feel uncomfortable for you
Most people don't know what to say
When someone criticizes them in a negative way
But how you respond says much about you
So respond in a positive way is the right thing to do

"Thank you very much for that today!"
"Is there anything else you'd like to say?"

Handling criticism is **not** an easy task
And these are some questions you need to ask?

"Could any of these things be really true?"
Because these criticisms seem to come right out of the blue
"Is this something I really need to know?"
Because being criticized is a blow to my ego
"Is there something I'm failing to see?"
"And is there **Someone** trying to get through to me?"

"Thank you very much for that today!"
"Is there anything else you'd like to say?"

Don't let your pride get in they way
And keep you from saying what you need to say.

Thank the person for that suggestion
And don't make an instant rejection
Don't make any excuses or become verbally abusive
Don't blame anyone or become very defensive
Listen and give it your consideration
Because accepting criticism can be a valuable education.

"Thank you very much for that today!"
"Is there anything else you'd like to say?"

VI. The OREO HNIC - ISI

Life on a Small Corporate Plantation

Before I left CDC, the Valley Forge Division became part of a new company called Computer Peripherals Incorporated (CPI). This new company was owned by CDC, NCR and another company. Everyone at Valley Forge became employees of CPI except me. My new job was to represent the parent, CDC, at the facility. This was an unacceptable situation for me so it gave me an additional reason to leave. I applied for a position of Assistant Vice-President of Marketing at the Institute for Scientific Information (ISI). I was told that over 500 people had sent their resumes in for that position. That was the first time I had gotten a job through the classifieds. This job was a change of pace for me.

ISI was a small corporation with sales of $10 million in 1972. Dr. Garfield who was a professor at University of Pennsylvania started the company. He recognized the need as an information scientist to have access to the latest information when you are doing research. So with $500 he started his first product called **Current Contents**. It was simply the table of contents of scientific journals put together in a book so that at a glance you could review hundreds of journals. You could then order the article from the library or ISI; a novel idea that caught on. ISI, of course, expanded to include other products. My boss, Dick Harris, was on a mission to try to bring a business mentality to the company. This company was run more like academia than a business. It was very prestigious in the company if you had your doctorate. Since the primary users of the information were researchers it was important that the company had people on staff who knew about researching information. I felt like a fish out of water there. I accepted the job because I wanted to leave CDC but stay in Philadelphia.

This company practiced valuing diversity long before it was popular. It was the first company that I had worked for that had a large number of women in management and other key positions. There were also three Black men in management including myself. It was a very interesting business but I had a difficult time keeping busy. I volunteered to take on more responsibility from any department. I was really my boss' "alter ego" and he really did not need someone with my capabilities in that job. I lasted for a year because I did not want to leave before then because it would look bad on my resume.

Put a Little Bit Back into the Pot

ISI was a fun place to work. There were after work parties and the wildest Christmas office party that I ever attended. Because a large part of the function was data entry, the company employed many females as data entry clerks and as managers. A Black man, *Tom Oreo*,* headed up this operation along with other responsibilities. He was a vice president, the highest-ranking Black in the company. He also had the largest department in the company reporting to him. We would talk from time to time because he was struggling with what his role should be as a Black man. He had a dilemma in trying to balance his career goals with his social responsibility. Should he adopt the attitude that "Profit is the name of the game" or did he have an obligation to try to help his brothers and sister?

One incident in particular triggered a discussion which really brought out how he felt about the situation. He stopped by my office one day to tell me that the company was opening another facility in a nearby suburban area. The main office was located in downtown Philadelphia. So I asked him why were they moving to suburbia? His response was that they were moving to suburbia because they were having a difficult time attracting qualified people to the office location in the city. The new facility was going to be a data entry center. By moving to a suburban residential area, the company felt that it would attract housewives who were looking for part time work. A strategy that made sense if that was the only reason. But *Tom** had another concern. He was very concerned about the influx of Blacks in his department since over half of the employees in his department were already Black. He felt that he had to do something about this before his department became predominately Black.

Tom was a very competent individual and highly respected by management but he had an identity problem with Blacks. I asked *Tom* if he felt the company was moving its facility to the suburbs because of the influx of Blacks in his department? He said, "absolutely not and that the primary reason was a matter of economics and nothing else."

Then, we started discussing the role of the Black man in middle management and executive level positions. I told *Tom* that I felt that a Black in management had a social responsibility as well as a business responsibility. On the contrary, *Tom* felt that although he would like to do something for his brothers and sisters, it was impractical for him to do. He said it was impossible for him to meet his company business commitments and help Blacks.

I was very disappointed to hear *Tom* say that and I told him so. I could not understand how a Black man could turn his back on his moral and social responsibility of helping his brothers and sisters get ahead. Was it really wrong for *Tom* to feel this way? Why shouldn't he just concentrate on looking out for himself? I knew that there were many people who felt the same way as *Tom* did. There are people who work very hard to make something of themselves and "made it" without having any concern about a moral or social responsibility. So why was I getting on *Tom*'s back? If he did not want to get involved why should I care?

I gave a lot of thought to those questions and although that happened in the early 1970s, I still have the same response today as I had then. Here is why I care. I care because the difference in opinions that *Tom* and I had represented the dilemma for the Black executive in industry now as well as then. *Tom* believed that if he became too concerned about the problems of Blacks, he would be identified by his White peers as a radical. He also felt that it was impractical to be "overly-concerned" about the problems of Blacks because he could not do anything to help the situation unless he worked full-time as a social worker or in some comparable capacity. *Tom* knew that because he was not concerned about the problems of Blacks, his Black coworkers knew this too. They also knew that he was married to a White woman which did not help his situation either. As a result, he alienated the friendship of most of the Blacks in the company.

Tom knew that he had been identified by Blacks as an OREO. A term derived from the OREO cookie meaning black on the outside and white on that inside. He was very uncomfortable being seen talking to Blacks in the halls especially talking to Blacks who reported to him. In his mind, this lowered his status as an executive. *Tom* knew that I did not agree with his attitude because I told him. So he put this question to me: "What could he do as a Black executive even if he wanted to do something?" Or better he said, "What can you do to help Blacks and still do your job as a manager?" This was *Tom*'s "gotcha" to me. I told *Tom* that he should do what he feels is best for himself. Further, I told him that every Black who has reached some level of success should *"Put a little bit back into the pot!"* He asked, "What do you mean by that?" I told him it meant this. As a Black, I should try to help at least one other Black to get ahead. This would help pay for the benefits I have reaped as a result of the marches and protests that helped us achieve the opportunities we have today.

Tom looked at me and laughed. He said. "You've got to be kidding because you don't owe anything to anybody!" In fact, he continued, "have you considered that you might not be able to do both? You might not be able to reach your professional career goals and at the same time be able to help Blacks because these goals are mutually exclusive." *Tom* might have been right in his assumptions, but it was not going to stop me from trying because I felt that I could make a difference. Maybe I will not change the world. But if I help at least one person and everyone else, who is in a position to do so, helps at least one person, then we will make some progress. Sometimes it is easier to make excuses for not doing something. For example, as demonstrated by his actions, Justice Clarence Thomas of the U.S. Supreme Court feels the same way as *Tom*. That is, "he doesn't owe Blacks anything because he feels he made it on his own."

Reflections on the Million Man March

By Aubrey B. Jones, Jr.

Racism is alive and well today
Although some people might dispute what I say
But let me tell you what was exciting for me
To be a part of the **Million Man March** on Washington, DC
I knew that the world would be watching us
So I said a prayer before I boarded the bus
I knew that some people did not want us to succeed
But the Brothers stood tall with a message to heed:

> *"Now is the time!*
> *Now is the time my brothers*
> *Now is the time to stand up and be a man*
> *Now is the time to stand up for your family and community*
> *Now is the time to be Strong, to be Black and to be Proud*
> *Now is the time!"*

As we marched down East Capitol Street
We were overwhelmed by the people that we'd meet
You could not help from being moved to tears
As the sisters along the way supported us with cheers
Everyone we'd meet greeted us with open arms and a smile
And you said to yourself, "if this is a dream, then don't wake me for a while"
There was something special and exciting about that day
People were warm and friendly and they all had this to say:

> *"Welcome brothers, glad you could come*
> *Looking good brothers, good to see you*
> *They said we couldn't do it but we did it anyhow!*
> *Be strong! Be Black! Be Proud!"*

The march did something for all Black men who attended
We let the world know that we had been offended
We said to the world that *"enough is enough"*
And that we refuse to put up with all that negative stuff
There was a feeling and spirit that permeated the crowd
It was Black men saying that *"we're Black and we're proud!"*
We shared in an experience that never happened in this country before
One Million Black Men standing together to say that we ain't going to take this stuff no more!
Now that the march is over where do we go from here?
We must go back to our communities and make it very clear
That there comes a time in a man's life
When he must stand up for his children and his wife
We can't depend on other people to do the job for us
We need to accept the challenge and do it for ourselves
We need to *"pull the coattails"* of the young people and *mentor* them on survival skills for this world today
We need to show the young people *how to do it* and not just *tell them* how they should do it. We need to *lead by example!*
We need to capture the energy, excitement and enthusiasm of the march and *energize others* in our communities
We need to *pull ourselves up by our roots* and regain the pride, self esteem and self respect that we once had

> *"Now is the time!*
> *Now is the time my brothers*
> *Now is the time to stand up and be a man*
> *Now is the time to stand up for your family and community*
> *Now is the time to be Strong, to be Black and to be Proud*
> *Now is the time! Now is the Time! Now Is the Time!"*
>
> *"Let's Do it! Let's Get Busy! Do It Now!*
>
> *Now is the Time!"*

Black is Beautiful

To *Tom* and others, I might sound like a dreamer or like I'm living in Utopia and not the USA. But I feel that everyone, both Blacks and Whites, will have to make a social commitment to solve the problems of our urban areas. There are no pat formulas and there is no magic to solve the socio-economic problems in America. Private Industry must make a commitment to use business methods and money to help tackle problems that local and federal governments have failed to solve. Here is where *Tom*, other Black managers and I can help. We can initiate thinking and concern of the business world on how to help solve some of the problems. We as Blacks can be role models to young brothers and sisters. We can mentor them, be big brothers and sisters to them, and we can talk to them and let them know that we care.

Am I a dreamer? Maybe so. But I can't agree with *Tom*'s position either. It really annoys me when a Black says or implies **"To hell with my brothers and sisters, I made it on my own so why can't they do the same thing?"** I would like to remind *Tom* and any other Black who feels the same way to remember something. Even though it might be true that *Tom* and others may have made it on their own merits, there were a lot of brothers and sisters who were beaten, jailed and even killed to open the doors for all Black people. Without Rosa Parks, Martin Luther king and others, the door to *Tom*'s executive suite would still be closed. Even the front door to the building where *Tom* is employed might still be closed to him.

There are no secret formulas for a Black man to succeed in a corporation. I felt that *Tom*'s chances of moving ahead were equally as good as or even better than mine. But if *Tom*, the OREO, makes it; he might say that he made it on his own merits and that he doesn't owe anything to anybody. But deep down he knows differently. He knows that he has given lip service to Whites and even some Blacks on integration and controversial social issues on his way to the top. We Blacks know that he is only concerned about being Black if he can in some way benefit from it. I really feel sorry for *Tom* because he still has to face the routine problems of getting the job done like any other manager. But in addition, he has to face the "political" decision of doing what he feels is the right thing to do without alienating both his Black and White coworkers. Although I don't agree with *Tom*'s philosophy, he should not be pressured by anyone to do something he truly does not believe in. I feel that a false commitment will do more harm than good.

Did *Tom*'s approach help him reach his career goals? Are corporations then and now looking for a Black who is a "White man in a Black Skin?" I can't really answer that question. But people in general feel more comfortable around people who are more like themselves. We saw some changes in the 1970s and realized that a few Blacks had reached top positions in the corporate world. The consensus among Blacks then was that in order to obtain the same opportunities in industry as Whites; we had to be exceptional. I feel that when you get right down to the competitive situations, promotions, high paying glamour jobs such as Sales and Fashion Design and even for some of the well paying white collar jobs, a Black has to be head and shoulders above Whites. He must be a Super Black! But even being a Super Black does not guarantee that he will get a job or promotion. There were cases where Blacks were given equal opportunities. I also knew of cases where companies hired or promoted Blacks of lesser qualifications to foster integration or to offer tokenism. But there were very few of these cases.

(Update: That was the way it was in the 60s and 70s. I'm not sure that many of the young Blacks feel the same way in 2005. Today, there are Blacks who are CEO's, presidents and in other top corporate positions. But also in 2005, many things will change if Congress and the courts succeed in doing away with some or all of Affirmative Action programs. We can't become complacent just because a few more doors have opened.)

Both *Tom* and I agreed on one thing. The quota system affects all Blacks who are employed directly or indirectly. In the 1960s and 1970s, many Blacks who were recently hired or promoted heard Whites say, "The only reason you got the job (or promotion) is because you are Black." This annoyed the hell out of us but we learned that such complaints came with the territory. I don't hear it as much today. My feeling is that it might have been true in some cases that being Black helped when seeking certain types of jobs. But who really wants a "Showcase" position? Sometimes it is difficult to determine during an interview whether or not a position is a "Showcase" position but it does not take long to find out after you're on the job. My final message for *Tom* was that money and prestige can only satisfy you for a short time. You still have to look at the man in the mirror. If you don't like what you see, then you better make some changes in your life.

In the early 1960s, I thought that I could get ahead if I did all of the "proper" things. That is, do things the way it was taught in school, or the way it was described in management textbooks, or the way my White colleagues "played the game." I knew that successful White executives followed the rule – "The best way to get ahead was to never become involved in political or controversial situations which put you in a bad position with management." Yes, some years ago, I was willing to "play the game" by the rules established for Whites by Whites. I was willing to put on my White attitude from nine to five and then revert to my Black attitude after five. This attitude was different for the OREO because he never reverted to the Black attitude unless it was advantageous for him. For the most part *Tom* kept his White attitude for twenty-four hours a day and seven days a week.

In the late 1960s, the Black revolution liberated me and I am very grateful for it. I have never considered myself a militant or even a troublemaker (although I am sure I will get some disagreements on this). I am an American who loves his country and I don't know of any other country that I would prefer to live. So why was I so happy about the Black Revolution that started in the sixties? Because **It set me free!** It made me proud of my heritage. I no longer felt that I had to emulate the White man to make it. Now, I could do my own thing whether it was wearing my hair in the Afro hairstyle, wearing a mustache or giving the Black power handshake. I could be myself for twenty four hours a day and still meet my professional commitments for my company.

Tom can learn something from the Black experience. He does not have to be ashamed of being Black anymore. He does not have to be afraid of being seen associating with other Blacks on the job. Nor does he have to be concerned that since he took over his department, it became 65% Black. He can forget about his concern that his department will be stereotyped as the "Black department." The Black experience can help build his self-confidence so that he can learn to cope with the situation. *Tom* can free himself from the turmoil he has been going through to find his identity. He can break out of the prison he has built for himself and *start being a man-A Black man*! He can step off the plantation. Come on *Tom*! I am pulling for you man. I guarantee that you will feel much better when you accept the fact that you're Black too and learn that it's not so bad. After all **Black is Beautiful!**

I'm An African-American
By Aubrey B. Jones, Jr.

My Roots Are In Africa
But I Was Born In America
My Roots Are In Africa
But I Was Born In America

*I*f You Look At The Color Of My Skin
You Can Tell That African Blood Flows Within.
If You Look At The Texture Of My Hair
You Can See My African Heritage There.
If You Look At My Dancing Feet
You Can See The Rhythm Of An African Beat.
If You Look At My Nose And My Mouth
Then There's Absolutely No Doubt.

My Roots Are In Africa
But I Was Born In America
My Roots Are In Africa
But I Was Born In America

I Must Admit That I've Never Been In Africa
And That I Know More About The Culture In America.
But That Doesn't Keep Me From Having Pride
In My African Heritage No Matter Where I Reside.
The Name "Black" Did Not Immediately Take Hold
Because Many Of Us Did Not Understand The Goal.
You See, "Black" Did Not Mean The Color Of Our Skin
But It Meant Our Culture, Our Heritage,
And Our Feelings Within.

*My Roots Are In Africa
But I Was Born In America
My Roots Are In Africa
But I Was Born In America*

Now That We Are Feeling Black And Proud
Here Comes Another Cry From The Crowd.
Some People Like The Name African-American
While Others Prefer To Be Called A Black-American.
Let Me Set The Record Straight
There's No Need For Long Debate.
African-American Shows The Right Connection
And That's The Reason It's The Right Selection.

*My Roots Are In Africa
But I Was Born In America
My Roots Are In Africa
But I Was Born In America*

If You Don't Want To Identify With The African Race
Then You're Entitled To Have Your Space.
But If You're Ashamed Of Who You Are
Then You're Probably Not Going To Get Too Far.
But You're Not Sure Of Your Identity, You Say?
Then Let Me Clear It Up For You Today.
If You Have Any African Blood Flowing In You
Then You're An African-American, Too!

Your Roots Are In Africa
But You Were Born An America
Your Roots Are In Africa
But You Were Born In America

Even If People Could Not Really See
The African Blood That Flows In Me.
I Would Tell Them If They Wanted To Know
About My African Heritage From Long Ago.
If They Would Ask Me Who I Am Today
I'm African-American Is What I'd Proudly Say.

My Roots Are In Africa
But I Was Born In America
My Roots Are In Africa
But I Was Born In America

I'm An African-American!

Back to the Fortune 500 Plantation

During the 1960s and 1970s, there was a lot of talk about equal opportunity employment. But many companies complained that they could not find any qualified Blacks. So when I started my search for a position, I decided to test the water to find out how serious the corporations were about hiring Blacks. I composed a letter addressed to the CEO's of six of the largest corporations. I started my letter like this:

> *"There is a lot of talk today about equal opportunity employment and I must admit that conditions have improved considerably over the past ten years. But as you know, there are very few Blacks who have made it to the top. I find myself in the position of many young Blacks with high aspirations but who are reluctant to seek positions which are nothing more than showcase or dead-end positions. Many companies complain that there are not enough qualified Blacks to handle top-level positions. This is true to some extent but there are some Blacks who are capable of handling top level positions. I am one of these Blacks"*

I also included a brief summary of my background and experience. Of the six letters I sent, I received responses from five and had one interview. The interview was with Philco Ford Consumer Products Division and I accepted a position as a Product Planning Manager for radios and televisions. The office was located in Blue Bell in the same plant that I worked in for my first job out of college. This job was different than any that I had before. One of the perks was each management level employee was able to lease a new Ford every year at a very modest fee.

I enjoyed working at Philco this go around but I was not able to stay there long. Philco, like many other American companies, was having trouble competing with the Japanese so they got out of that business and I was laid off after a little over a year. I was there long enough, however, to pick up some new skills and to learn about another industry. When this door closed another one opened - I was blessed! I found a better job and was working within two weeks. My next job was a major step up. I finally made Director level. I was offered a position of Director of Strategic Planning at Sperry Remington Office Products. Sperry Remington's building was located right next to Philco Ford in Blue Bell. One of the reasons that I was able to get a job so fast was that I knew someone in personnel who used to work with me at CDC.

I learned several lessons from working at Philco-Ford. (1) Don't burn your bridges because you never know when you might want to return. Philco-Ford was my first job out of college as an Engineer. Although this was a different division, I was still rehired. (2) Keep abreast of the market for you skills. If your skills need to be upgraded or expanded then do it. And (3) networking works! Because I knew someone at Sperry, I was able to get a new position within a short period of time.

VII. Working On Sperry's Corporate Plantation

Do You Have a Chip on Your Shoulder?

Sperry Remington was an office products company. It introduced its first typewriter in 1873. In addition to typewriters it offered a complete line of office products worldwide including copiers, word processors and accounting machines. Most of its product line was very old and Remington was gradually getting out of the manufacturing business. To my knowledge, I was the first Black who had ever been hired in a management position at corporate headquarters. As part of the hiring process, I had to pass several psychological tests and was interviewed by a number of people. One of the interviewers was the vice president of personnel. He had been working for the company for over thirty years and his job was to try to determine if I could fit in with the old-line management of Sperry Remington. I was forewarned, by several people who wanted me to be hired, that the vice- president was somewhat apprehensive about hiring a Black Director.

He was a crafty old guy who used his years of experience to develop questions that kept me on my toes. During the interview, he asked me to explain how I would handle certain hypothetical situations if they came up. Then he asked me how I felt about being the only Black on the management team. This was an easy response for me. At this time, I had over ten years experience working in White male corporate environment. I told him that I felt very comfortable in that environment and did not anticipate any problems I could not handle. He wanted me to be more specific on how I would handle a crisis if it occurred on the job. Specifically, he wanted to know what I would do if I was confronted by one of my White coworkers who might not like me or just wanted to give me a hard time.

I said to him, "The first thing is to be cool and evaluate the circumstances surrounding the situation." To evaluate the situation, I use the checklist approach. When someone challenges me, or becomes negative with me, I try not to take it personally and I usually step back and ask myself a few questions. "Did I do something to cause this person to react negatively toward me? Are there work related circumstances that might cause this person to respond the way that he did? Is the person just having a bad day? And the final question is simply: *'Maybe?' Maybe* that person is a racist!" If I think that a person's action is a result of a racist attitude, I will not respond and try to walk away from it. If it is a racist response, I used the approach that some old folks used: *"I see but I don't see and I hear but I don't hear!"* In short, I will not dignify a racist response with a comment. I will just leave it alone unless there is a threat of physical harm to me or a threat to my family.

My candor intrigued the Vice President but he wanted to know how I could tell if a person was a racist. I told him that most Black folks have a sixth sense about this. We had developed a sixth sense to survive over the years. We had to learn to read White people like a book. We had to identify friend or foe or whom could we trust. To assimilate into a white society, we had to learn the rules of the game. Certainly, some Blacks might overreact to some situations and accuse people as being racists when they may not be. But the secret is not to react to every situation that you think is due to a racist attitude. It's a judgment call and a survival strategy. When you learn that you have the power to rise above negatives and to deal with the challenges in your life, you will ultimately succeed. That is, if you can hang in there long enough. My response blew the vice-president's mind. I had never given anyone this kind of response before, but I knew this was a chess match and he wanted to see if he could checkmate me.

Near the end of my interview, the vice-president asked me very casually: *"Do you have a chip on your shoulder?"* I looked at him, smiled and said, *"Yes I do, but it used to be a log!"* He thought that was very funny, we both laughed, and the interview was over. After I thought about my answer, about the chip on my shoulder, it probably best described me at that time. I said it as a joke but it was really true. After living in the south and having to deal with segregation, I had come a long way in improving my self-esteem and my self-confidence. I tried not to let things get to me, and if they did, I would not react to them or dignify a negative situation with a comment. I had learned to focus on the more important things in life and refused to let anyone bring me down because of his or her negative actions. The vice president told me that I came across in the interview as a person who could handle himself in almost every situation. I started with Remington on April 15, 1974.

Introduction to the Poem "Pull Yourself Up by Your Roots!"

As African-Americans, we have come a long way.
And for those who might have forgotten how far we've come,
I just want to remind you that we accomplished a lot more in the past with a lot less than what we have available to us today.
I just want to remind you *not* to give up no matter how big the obstacle might appear to be.
I just want to remind you not to look *outside* for help but to look *inside*.
I know that there will be times in your life when you will get down. But the secret is if you get down, is not to stay down.
If you get down, *"Pull Yourself up By Your Roots!"*

Pull Yourself Up By Your Roots!
By Aubrey B. Jones Jr.

If anyone ever implies or tells you
that you can't do something because you're Black.
Remember that your roots are strong and deep
and that you can't be held back.
Remember that your roots are in Africa
and that you survived and overcame a lot of things in America.

You survived slavery, segregation, discrimination
and many other *cruel indignities.*
You survived riding on the back of the bus, drinking out of
separate water fountains and living in **segregated** communities.

You *learned* despite attending *segregated* schools
where you had to use *old, ragged,* "*hand me down*" books,
discarded by the white schools.
You *learned* despite using *inadequate* facilities
and learning materials because you had the " *will*" *to learn*
instilled in you by teachers who really cared about you.

You *overcame* major obstacles to go to college
and became doctors, lawyers, teachers, engineers and
other professionals.
You *accepted the challenge* to start your own businesses
when the white-owned establishments *refused* to serve you.

Remember how far you've come and that the struggle is never over.
Remember that life is full of obstacles and challenges and if you give up every time you're faced with a challenge you'll never accomplish anything.
When an obstacle seems like an impossible situation, *Pull yourself up by your roots* and approach it with a strong faith and determination

Pull yourself up by your roots and remember that you did it before and you can do it again.
Pull yourself up by your roots and regain the pride, self-esteem and self-respect that you once had.
Pull yourself up by your roots and regain your strong faith and belief in *GOD* because *all things are possible through HIM.*

Pull Yourself up by Your Roots!

Is It Because I'm Black?

My boss, *Earl The-Pearl* was an enigma to me and everyone else. Everyone thought that he was wealthy and that he had a special relationship with the president of Sperry. He never tried to clarify it for anyone because he enjoyed having people think he had a connection with the president. I thought I had a special relationship with *Earl The-Pearl* too until I found out differently later. The position of Director of Strategic Planning had been viewed in the past as a place where you put discarded executives out to pasture. The person who held that position before me was a vice president who was waiting to retire. During my interview, I made it very clear that I would not accept that position unless I had the authority to interact with the department heads to develop a real strategic plan. And the plan, when completed, would not just be a well written document sitting on the shelf but we would use it and that I would have a role in its implementation.

One of the first things that I did as Director was to set up a one-on-one meeting with each of the product managers to get a feel for where we were in the product life cycles. This was a huge task because Remington had hundreds of products. So we set up a *"war room"* to display a listing of all the products and the status of each one. We used color codes so that we could tell the status at a glance. I asked each manager several basic questions, like: "When was the product introduced, when was the last time it was modified and what were their plans for new products?" After all of the information was gathered, we were ready to do an analysis and make recommendations.

Everything went well for the first few months. We completed the strategic and development plan process with specific recommendations for the division. Sperry Remington was a $300 million division with marginal profits. One of the problems the division had was that its accounting system did not permit it to determine profitability by product line. As a result, there were a number of products that were being sold unprofitably. Over the years, Sperry Corporation had used Sperry Remington as the cash cow. That is, it pulled out all of the cash (profits) to invest in new computer products and left virtually no money to invest in office products. All of these things ultimately spelled doom for Remington. The first step towards doomsday occurred after I was there a little over a year when Remington was integrated into Sperry Univac and Remington was renamed the Office Equipment Division of Sperry Univac. Along with this integration, a number of manufacturing facilities were closed down. "The hand was writing on the wall" and I knew that my job was going away.

To be proactive, I met with Sperry Univac's Vice president of Personnel, *Bob NoAction*. I asked him if I should be looking for a job outside of Sperry. He told me absolutely not because he felt a suitable position could be found for me in Univac. In the meantime I was unassigned. I had absolutely nothing to do but come to work, go home and pick up my paycheck. After a while it became a little embarrassing for me because everyone would ask me, *"Have you heard anything yet?"* This went on for about four months. I became very bored and frustrated. I had not heard a thing from personnel. I knew something was up one day when *Bob NoAction* passed right by me in the hall and did not speak or even look at me. *Earl The-Pearl,* my boss, called me in his office and told me that he had heard that I was going to be laid off. He told me that someone said to him, *"You went out and hired yourself a Black Director, now you figure out what to do with him?"* Earl said that he did not know what to tell me to do. So since I had nothing to lose, I decided it was time to write a letter to the president who was, at that time, Mr. G.G. Probst. Here is a copy of the letter I sent to him.

(Letter to President Of Univac)

9999 E. Sedgwick St.
Philadelphia, Pa. 19150

April 14, 1975

Mr. G. G. Probst
President
Sperry Univac
P.O. Box 500
Blue Bell, Pa, 19422

Dear Mr. Probst:

When I made the decision a year ago to come to Sperry Remington, I did so for the following reasons:

1. It afforded me the opportunity to enter a Fortune 500 corporation at a position which was both interesting and challenging to me.

2. It appeared that Remington had some Product lines with the potential to make it a major competitor in the marketplace.

3. I saw an opportunity to use my Engineering, Planning, Marketing and Program Management background and experience to help Sperry Remington meet its short and long term objectives.

4. I know I have the background and experience to be a top executive in any corporation, if given the opportunity, and Sperry Rand appeared to be the kind of corporation where this opportunity existed.

In a very short period of time at Sperry Remington, I made a number of significant accomplishments. For example:

- *Generated Planning Guidelines for the Division.*

- *Organized and chaired the Planning council.*

- *Reviewed each Product Line with its respective Product Manager and established product life cycles, short and long term goals and product profitability. This information was made available for management information and action. It was also displayed in the Chart Room. (Note: None of the above was ever accomplished prior to this.)*

- *Completed the appraisal for Sperry Remington for FY 76 through FY 80 which included a factual S.W.O.T. (strengths, weaknesses, opportunities and threats) analysis together with pragmatic recommendations for the division.*

- *Organized a Planning and Product Management Group to handle WPS and OCS product lines after the integration of Remington and Univac.*

- *Developed a long range business plan for WPS with the objectives of reducing the corporations short term exposure and also establishing a product and marketing base for long term growth in WPS.*

The above is just a sample of some of the accomplishments that I made in a very short period of time at Sperry Remington.

I realize that the decision to integrate Remington with Univac and to divest some of Remington's product lines was probably a tough decision for you. But what I cannot rationalize is how a person with my capability, background and experience can be left in limbo.

I have been left in limbo for almost four months. I have no work assignments and I do not know what my future is with Sperry Rand. I was told over and over by Earl The-Pearl*, Mike Banton* and others, that I have a good track record. To date, however, I have not been told anything about my next assignment.

I am a very action-oriented person and because no one seemed to know my destiny, I initiated some action. About five or six weeks ago, I called Mr. Bob NoAction* and requested to meet and talk with him about my future. He agreed to do this. During our meeting, I asked him if I should be looking for another position outside of the company. He reassured me that he felt that a suitable position could be found for me within the corporation. To date, I have not heard from Mr. NoAction or his staff.

I have tried over and over to rationalize why there is no opportunity for me in Sperry Rand, but I cannot seem to come up with a logical explanation. Why do you think I am difficult person to place in Sperry Rand? **Is it because I am Black?**

I regret having to write to you about this matter but it is important to me to know why I will have to leave Sperry Rand to seek the opportunity which I thought existed here.

I have enclosed a copy of my career highlights that will give you some additional insight to my background and experience.

Very truly yours,

Aubrey B. Jones Jr.

* Not the real name here.

The Pen is Mightier than the Sword

After not hearing anything for over four months, I received a response to my letter within a week. Mr. Probst sent me short memo acknowledging receipt of my letter and alerting me that I could expect to hear from *Mr. Noaction* or his designee in the near future. According to sources, *Mr. NoAction* was not too happy about me writing to the president. I was told that *Bob NoAction* mentioned to someone that, *"He was caught with his pants down."* It's amazing how fast things move sometimes when the order comes down from the top. Within a short period of time, I was reassigned as the Director of Strategic Planning for the Office Equipment Division of Univac (The Remnants of Sperry Remington). I reported to *Earl The-Pearl* again, but I did a lot of work for the Vice President and General Manager of that Division, *Al Hero*.

Al was a great guy to work for because he was easy going and allowed me to take on a lot more responsibilities. One of my duties was to write the Division's monthly report based on the input from *Al's* staff. Having access to the staff reports put me in a very good position to know what was going on in the division. From this experience, I learned that when you stand up against the system as I did; there is a price to pay. I had to regain the trust and support of my management. I know that it was the right thing to do because I had nothing to lose. If I had not written the letter, I would probably have been laid off.

Al Hero gave me the opportunity to use my skills and add some value to the division. All I ever wanted was an opportunity to demonstrate what I could do. In 1977, *Al* told me that he had recommended me to participate in a management conference in Hilton Head, South Carolina. He told me that I would receive my official invitation from *Bob NoAction*. This management conference was held periodically for all of the top managers of all divisions of Sperry Corporation. They also used this conference to give young mangers the opportunity for visibility by allowing them to make presentations to this group. When *Al* told me about my pending invitation, he also told me not to mention it to *Earl the-Pearl* yet because he did not know about it.

After I received my invitation, I was teamed with two panel members from other divisions of Sperry. We were assigned a senior vice president as our coach and mentor. We had to prepare to present on the topic: "The Office of the Future." This was a very hot topic in the seventies and Sperry wanted to investigate what role, if any, it should play in this emerging market. *Neil Goodguy*, Vice President for Product Strategy and Requirements, was our mentor. I met with my panel members along with *Neil* to develop our presentation. John, a technically oriented person from Salt Lake City, and Mary Lou, a sales person from Washington, D.C and I representing the office equipment division comprised the panel. We worked very well together and decided to use a cartoon-oriented approach to help the audience understand what office automation was all about. We put together a 45-minute presentation that covered everything you needed to know about office of the future together with some recommendations for Sperry.

We rehearsed the presentation a number of times to make certain that everything was perfect. I was the chairperson for our panel which meant I had to give the introduction and the closing remarks. After *Neil Goodguy* reviewed the presentation with us, he told us to spice it up. So I came up with an idea for my part, but it would be a little risky. Sometimes when you tell a joke or try to be funny it can backfire on you. But one advantage of being Black was that I could afford to take a risk. I felt that many of the people probably were not expecting much from me anyway so if I bombed it was no big deal. But if I pulled it off, as I felt I would, it would be a pleasant surprise for everyone.

Mr. J. Paul Lyet, the chairman, Mr. Probst, the president, and most of the senior management of the Sperry Corp were in the audience. When it was my turn to speak, I said the following. "Good morning! Welcome to the first EEO panel on Office Automation. When *Bob NoAction* asked me to be a member of this panel, I told him I did not know anything about Office Automation. And he said, *that's alright Aubrey nobody expects you to know anything anyhow. All we want you to do is to add some color to this conference."* The audience laughed and I broke the ice. I turned a perceived weakness into a strength. Each of the panelists performed well. I closed with a poem and these remarks.

> "In closing I would like to steal a page from the world's greatest salesman. And without a doubt that's Muhammad Ali. And if he was here, he'd close with a poem. And the poem would probably go like this: Sperry Univac is the greatest. The Number one company of latest but what about IBM, Burroughs and Honeywell. They can go to hell because in office automation we'll have the latest and show the world that we're the greatest!"

Afterwards, we handed out buttons that said, "Sperry Univac is the Greatest!" The presentation was a hit.

There was a good reason *Al Hero* told me not to mention to *Earl The-Pearl* that I had been invited to go to Hilton Head. *Earl The-Pearl* was not invited. When I received my official invitation, I told *Earl The-Pearl* that I had been invited. As my boss I felt he should know about it. He said he knew about it but did not know whether or not they would let me go because of my age and other reasons. I asked "what other reasons?" He said,

"Because you are Black!" He also told me that I should not tell anyone that I was going because they would be upset with me. He was upset because he was not invited to participate. The reason he mentioned my age was because I was 40 years old at the time and he said that normally they pick the "young Turks."

After the presentation, I felt the wrath of *"Earl The-Pearl."* He told me that "OA" was his baby and he didn't want any M____F_____ running around him or trying to undercut him. That was the furthest thing from the truth and he knew it. He was probably upset over the exposure I was getting because the presentation went so well. He wanted to be the focal point for "OA" because it was the future of the Office Equipment Division. I was also invited to travel to Japan to make the entire presentation on "OA" by myself to our Japanese subsidiary.

We spent two weeks in Japan making presentations in Tokyo, Kyoto and Yokohama. One of the highlights of my presentation was that I delivered my introduction in Japanese. In Blue Bell, a Japanese colleague wrote out my introduction phonetically. Before I traveled to Japan, I practiced my presentation so that I could read my introduction well enough to be understood by the audience. I also had an interpreter who had a copy of the presentation. I would speak and he would interpret in Japanese for the audience. In Tokyo, we presented in a theater style auditorium with about 600 people. During my introduction, I said in Japanese. *"Good morning ladies and gentlemen. It is indeed a pleasure for me to speak to you on the office of the future."* After I said that in Japanese, I said in English, *"I'm sorry but that's all of the Japanese I know and so I will have to do the rest in English."* I received a standing ovation because of my effort in Japanese. The Japanese were very gracious hosts.

Because of my success with OA, my relationship with *Earl The-Pearl* deteriorated. He reorganized the department and did not include me in his new organization. He said that he did not create a position for me because I asked to leave the group. The irony of the entire situation was that I had been one of his biggest supporters. I trusted *Earl The-Pearl* and told him a lot of personal things over time that I should not have told him. But I made an erroneous assumption that he was secure enough not to see me as a threat. *I was wrong, I made a mistake and I paid a price.* As it turned out, things worked out better. I transferred to *Neil Goodguy's* group, Product Strategy and Requirements, in Sperry Univac Computer Division.

You Receive Much More than You Give

Neil was a wonderful person to work for. He was smart man with a dry sense of humor. Perhaps because he was Jewish, he had an appreciation of what I had to go through in Sperry. *Neil* encouraged me to get involved in community related organizations. He was the one who suggested that I volunteer for PRIME (Philadelphia Regional Introduction of Minorities to Engineering). He approved my trips to participate in the National Urban League and BEEP (Black Executive Exchange Program) Conferences. BEEP was a program where Black professionals would visit historically Black colleges and serve as role models and visiting professors for a day or even longer periods. I traveled to many of the Historically Black Colleges to give exposure to the students on what was happening in the corporate world from a Black's perspective. Another benefit of belonging to BEEP was that it gave me an opportunity to network with Black professionals from other corporations.

Whereas BEEP focused on college level students, PRIME focused on students from grades 7 to 12. The goal of PRIME was to introduce more minorities to careers in engineering. At that time, Univac was one of 40 organizations in the Philadelphia area participating in PRIME. I was assigned to work with Leeds

Middle School in Philadelphia. When I volunteered to be Univac's PRIME representative, I agreed under the condition that I would have Univac's full support to do whatever was necessary to have the best program in the city. There were 70 seventh and eighth graders in the PRIME program at Leeds. On Wednesday afternoons and on Thursday mornings, I met with the students. Becoming computer literate at an early age is very important for students who are interested in engineering as a career. In 1980, personal computers had not become the ubiquitous devices they are today. Teaching computer literacy involved getting the students and teachers to feel comfortable using the computer.

All of the early PCs could be programmed in the BASIC programming language. But most people did not know how to program nor did they want to learn. So we decided to teach the students how to program in BASIC. Tandy Radio Shack donated eleven computers to the school and I developed the curriculum for teaching the students. All of the students learned how to write simple programs in BASIC. At Leeds, our theme was *"I Can DO It Too!"* We taught the students more than just how to program a computer. We used the computer to help build the students self-esteem and to teach them discipline. The computer is unforgiving. If you don't follow instructions when writing a program, it won't work. It could be frustrating at times but the students hung in there. When they finished, they felt real good about themselves. Not only did the students become computer literate but they also improved their self-esteem.

I believe that whenever you help someone you will get it back much more than you give. One story in particular sticks out in my mind when I think about working with the PRIME students. When we gave the first quiz only two students failed. I was very interested in learning why anyone failed the quiz. One girl failed because she did not follow instructions. The other student who failed was a young man named Daryl. I met with Daryl in the school's library so I could ask him in private how he felt about the quiz. But before I could get started, he began to cry. This caught me completely off guard because I was not expecting this type of reaction. After calming him down, I told him that I just wanted to know what areas he found the most difficult so that I could help him. Daryl told me that he did not understand any of it. I knew that was not totally true so I continued to probe a little. What I learned was that the other students always teased him because he was small for his age. As a result he had very low self-esteem and a lot of self-doubt. He just felt he was not capable of learning about computers.

At the time of the first Quiz, we did not have the computer room completely set up so that all of the students could get enough hands on time. We did have one computer set up in the back of the class and I suggested that Daryl stay around after school to get some additional practice. To make a long story short, Daryl took my suggestion and became very proficient in using the computer. He became so confident that he was even helping other students who were stuck on a problem. His self-esteem went way up. He received the "Giant Stride Award" during an assembly because he learned the most in the shortest time. When the students from the Leeds PRIME program graduated and moved up to high school they had the jump on most students when it came to understanding and using computers. Occasionally, I would see some of my former students in the mall or other places and they would tell me how much the course helped them. To me that was my biggest reward to know that I had helped someone.

My goal was to teach the course for one year and then train the teachers on how to deliver it. I had two excellent teachers working with me on the program - Dr. Bill Metz, a science teacher, and Mrs. Alice Jordan, a math teacher. In late 1979, I attended a computer show and stopped by the booth of Hayden Book Company. While I was browsing, looking for some books that might be helpful to our program, I met Irv Lopatin, the General Manager. During our discussion, I told him what I was doing at Leeds Middle school. And he said to me, "Aubrey, we are always looking for new materials for a book, let us take a look at what you have done so far." I was very excited and immediately asked, "When do you want to do it?" A few weeks later, he sent his editorial director, Mike Violano, to visit me. After he reviewed all of the overheads that we used for teaching, he said, "Let's do it! I think we have the makings of a good product."

Although I was excited about the idea of publishing a book, I never expected that it would sell as many copies as it did. As it turned out, my book, *"I Speak BASIC to My TRS-80"* was the right product, for the right time. Many teachers were frustrated in trying to find material simple enough for them to understand and easy enough for students to use as texts. *"I Speak BASIC to My TRS-80"* provided the schools with everything they needed to teach a course except the computers. There was a teacher's manual with annotations and answers, a student's text and quizzes on spirit duplicating masters. Recognizing that most of the schools in the country used Apple computers, I wrote a version entitled: *"I Speak BASIC to My Apple"* which turned out to be my best seller. I ended up with nine versions of the book series to cover all of the major personal computers used in the schools. Over 250,000 copies of the books were sold throughout the country. A real Blessing!

Time to Move On

It was very obvious to me that I had hit the "glass ceiling" in Sperry Univac. There was no way that I would be able to advance in a company where at that time I was probably the highest ranking Black in the company. And the only reason I reached that level at Sperry Univac was because I slipped in through the "back door." That is, I was hired by Remington and because it became a part of Univac and because of my letter to the president, I was able to survive. When I was moved to *Neil Goodguy's* group, my title was changed to Staff Consultant. Regardless of the assignments that I was given, I always made the best of them. My most significant accomplishment was my work on the Sperrylink Office Automation System. This was Univac's entry into the office automation market. Univac was in a position to really capture a large share of that market but it did not have competitive hardware at that time. Univac had a commitment to large mainframes and any OA product that was introduced had to be tied to a mainframe to protect its customer base. By requiring the workstations to be tied to a mainframe to operate, the entry cost for a new customer to OA was very high. If you were an existing customer and had capacity on your existing system then OA was much more cost effective.

We built a prototype system in Blue Bell that was used to demonstrate electronic mail, word processing and other functions that are commonplace today. The problem with Sperrylink was that the workstations were too big and bulky to sit on a desk and the costs were prohibitive. At that time the workstations did not have a graphics capability although PCs like the Radio Shack TRS-80 had it. When there is a new project with potential in the house, people come out of the woodwork to become involved. Despite my background and experience with office products and computers, I was not assigned one of the key positions on the project. However, I did bring a user's perspective to the project and used my communications skills to help develop user friendly manuals and other materials.

Another time, I was assigned to a communications task force that had the responsibility of reducing the number of Univac computer operating systems from five to one or two. Most of the people on the task force were senior level technical people from different organizations in the company. *Neil Goodguy* had assigned me to the task force because of my planning skills but most of the other members did not understand why I was on the task force. They assumed that I could add little value to this elite team. It was true that I did not have a strong software background but what they did not know was that I had a strong systems and planning background.

This was a long-term assignment and, as the project progressed, some of the members noticed my value to the team. For example, when they would become stuck on an issue I knew the right questions to ask to get them moving. And my biggest contribution was helping to organize and prepare the final report for presentation to the president's staff. We had developed a plan on how to reduce the number of operating systems to two, and next we had to sell the recommendation to the executive committee. The chairperson of the task force commented in a meeting that he was glad I was there because I was the only real planner on the team. This project turned out to be a very good assignment for me because it gave me visibility and allowed me demonstrate what I could do if given the opportunity. I worked on a number of other projects at Univac that helped develop my background in communications and medium sized systems.

A search firm, who was looking to fill a position at RCA, contacted me. I was not the least bit interested in joining RCA because I had always regarded it as very unprofessional in its practices. Further, it had the reputation of being a real old-line company with a blue-collar attitude especially towards Blacks. So when the headhunter called me I told him I was not interested. But he kept trying to persuade me to take the interview. He said the position was a perfect match for my background and experience. So I agreed to meet with the Vice

President of Strategic Planning, *Phil Carefree*, for dinner. After dinner, he asked me if I would come to the office to meet with the President of RCA Service Company and other key members of his staff. I agreed to do so. But after the meetings, I was not convinced that I wanted to work for RCA Service Company. One of the people who interviewed me, the CFO (Chief Financial Officer), even asked me sarcastically, "why do you want to leave Univac to come to RCA." And I told him that I was not sure if I wanted to come to RCA. Finally, I was asked to travel to New York to meet with the group vice-president.

I was impressed with the group VP and he gave me a reason to consider coming to RCA. He told me that most of the senior management team was ready for retirement and that they did not have enough qualified people internally who could fill the soon to be vacant slots. He also told me that by coming in as Director of Strategic Planning, I would have an opportunity to get up to speed real fast and to know all of the key players. Another reason he wanted me to join the company was that they did not have any Blacks in key management positions in RCA Service Company. This looked like it might be a good opportunity for me to crash through the "glass ceiling." After some negotiating, RCA Service Company made me an offer I could not refuse.

During the negotiations however, I was told that I would be eligible for the executive bonus. So when I asked them to put it in writing, I was told that they could not do that because the eligibility list is determined each year and that anyone who receives a bonus must get a letter from the Chairman of RCA. This seemed a little strange to me but it was true as I learned later. I told them that I had been burnt before on an executive bonus because Sperry Remington also promised me that I would be eligible for a bonus. Sperry never put it in writing and I did not receive a bonus. RCA understood why I was reluctant to accept their word so they proposed to provide me some up front money as a show of good faith. So they put in writing that I would receive a signing bonus and another bonus of equal amount on my one-year anniversary. In addition, I did receive an executive bonus each year thereafter. This was the first job that I received a salary plus an executive bonus. It was by far the most money I had ever made. But as I soon learned, money does not necessarily bring job satisfaction.

Ownership

By Aubrey B. Jones, Jr.

Take a look at yourself and what do you see
Are you the kind of person that you want to be?
Take a look at yourself and what is your view
Are you taking advantage of all the opportunities for you?
Take a look at yourself and if you still feel okay
Then you've passed the first test and you're well on your way.

> *If you want to win*
> *You must start within*
> *You can do it too!*

Suppose there's something that you really want to do
Then you should go for it and don't let anything stop you.
When an obstacle seems like an impossible situation
Just approach it with faith and determination.
When you're faced with a real challenge today
Hang in there and don't let anyone lead you astray.
So don't blame others when things don't go right
Accept the challenge and put up a good fight.

Don't look for reasons to *concede*
But rather look for ways of how to *succeed.*
You must take *ownership* of your situation
And be *responsible* for your destination.
Don't let people play a mind game on you
By telling you what you can and cannot do.
I believe that you can do what you want to do
All it takes now is for *you to believe it too!*

> *If you want to win*
> *You must start within*
> *You can do it too!*

VIII. Working on RCA Service Company's Plantation

It's a Dirty Job but a Slave has to Do It!

RCA Service Company was a cash cow division for RCA Corporation. It was close to $1 billion in revenue with high profit margins. It was also a very unsophisticated company in terms of systems, policies, procedures and management. The Service Company had three primary markets: Consumer, Commercial and Government. A major source of income came from Consumer service contracts for radios and televisions. But this source was drying up because as televisions became more reliable and less expensive, people stop buying service contracts. So the Service Company had to look in other areas for growth such as Office Automation. A major reason why they hired me was to help them get into that market.

After just being with the company a short period of time, I attended an all day manager's meeting which was held at a local hotel. At this meeting one of the young rising stars, *Earl Cola*, presented his plans for RCA Service Company to move into the Office Automation (OA) market. Just before the meeting started, the president of RCA Service Company pulled me aside and told me to ask *Earl Cola* a lot of questions. He wanted me to challenge him and play the role of "devils advocate." Now I thought this was a very strange request because this was my first meeting with the management team. I was a new kid on the block, who happened to be Black, and during my debut I was going to challenge the "Golden Boy?" I did not like it but I did it anyway. After listening to *Earl Cola*'s presentation for a little while, it was obvious to me that it had very little substance. But most of the management staff did not have the knowledge to challenge what was being presented. And even if they did, they probably would have not done anything to embarrass *Earl*. Evidently the president was suspicious that the plan was weak but he did not want to be the one to attack *Earl* in the meeting. So he picked me to do his dirty work.

As I began to ask *Earl Cola* simple questions, it was apparent that he did not have answers. He tried to dance around the questions but I would not let him get away with it. I kept homing in on specifics. I could see *Earl* becoming very frustrated and annoyed with me. I could also see the looks I was getting from the rest of the staff. I could hear them thinking, "Where did this guy come from?" and "Who is he trying to impress?" Unbeknownst to them, I was following orders. During the break there were some off hand remarks made like, "*Earl* who's your friend?" I really felt bad for *Earl* because he was not prepared to make a presentation. He was an excellent sales person but he had very limited marketing and planning skills. He had a vision of what he wanted to do but he really did not know how to make his vision a reality. For obvious reasons, *Earl Cola* and I never really hit it off after that. Later, I did tell him the truth on why I asked all of the questions. That might have helped a little but not much because the damage was already done. **"It's a dirty job but a slave has to do it."**

The Boss' Secretary

In most companies I have worked for, the boss' secretary is the informal second in command. Many of them have powers delegated to them by the boss who makes them much more than just a secretary. This is okay except when the secretary abuses that position and relationship with her boss. Probably no better example of how a secretary abuses her position than the president's secretary at RCA Service Company. Most of the other secretaries in the office were afraid of her. Even members of the president's staff were afraid to cross her. She was always very polite to me and basically I did not have a problem until she chastised my secretary. My secretary, Jeaneane, was one of the nicest people you would want to meet. She had excellent secretarial skills and would do anything to help anyone. I do not remember all of the specifics of what happened but I do remember returning to my office one day finding my secretary in tears. Quite naturally, I wanted to know what was going on but she did not want to tell me. I learned later that she had a confrontation with the president's secretary.

So later on during the day I saw the president's secretary, *Ms. Prissy*, in my area talking to another manager. I approached her to ask her what had happened between her and Jeneane. She got upset at me for asking her about the situation and stormed out of the office. The next thing I knew, my boss, *Phil Carefree*, comes into my office and tells me to go down and apologize to *Ms. Prissy*. I said, "Apologize for what?" He said *Ms. Prissy* is very upset and if I don't go down and apologize, she will cry to the president, *Admiral Stern*, and there will be hell to pay for everyone. I said, "You've got to be kidding! I don't have anything to apologize for, and in fact, I have a witness to what I said to her. I only asked her a question out of my concern for Jeneane." He said "I don't care about the details just go down and apologize to her."

I told him, "This is where I draw the line and if you want to fire me because I won't apologize for something I didn't do then go right ahead!" Well, he was not real happy about that, but this was one time *Ms. Prissy* was not going to have her way. After the incident, *Ms. Prissy* stopped speaking to me. She would walk right pass me as if I did not exist. If I was talking to other people when she passed, she would speak to them and ignore me. This went on until the president was replaced some six months later. I never got any flack from the president on this incident.

Now *Ms. Prissy* could be one of the nicest people you wanted to meet if she wanted something from you. It was amazing to me how everyone patronized her. She would come into the office area expecting compliments from other secretaries on how she looked that day. Nobody dared tell her the truth so they told her what they thought she wanted to hear. She always addressed me as "Mr. Jones" until she stopped speaking to me.

When the new president came on board and it was announced that I would be reporting to him, I decided that it was time to have a chat with *Ms. Prissy*. So I asked her to stop by my office one day and she did. I told her that it was very apparent to me and everyone else that she had been avoiding me for the past few months and we could not continue working this way. I also said that since I would be going in and out of the president's office to meet with him periodically, we needed to work out our differences. She told me that I humiliated her in front of other people when I asked her what happened between her and my secretary. I told her it was never my intention to humiliate or hurt her but all I wanted to do was just try to find out what happened. I also told her that I would have done the same thing for her if she was my secretary. After we talked for a while, we declared a truce and *Ms. Prissy* started speaking to me again. That was the one and only time I had a run in with the boss' secretary, *Ms. Prissy*. The lesson here is to watch out for people like **Ms. Prissy**!

Work it Out!
(Conflict Resolution)
By Aubrey B. Jones, Jr.

* Work it out!
Stop, Think, Listen and Talk
And work it out
Because it doesn't have to be that way.

Work it out!
Stop, Think, Listen and Talk
And work it out
Because it doesn't have to be that way.

Do you know what you need to do
If your friend or partner picks a fight with you?

Work it out!
Stop, Think, Listen and Talk
And work it out
Because it doesn't have to be that way.

Suppose someone:
    Jumps in your face and invades your space.
    Says something about you that you know is not true.
    Calls you a name or **disrespects** you during a game.
    Takes something from you right "out of the blue"

(Chorus)

Don't bite, don't kick, don't scream or holler
Here are some rules for you to follow.

Work it out!
Stop, Think, Listen and Talk
And work it out
Because it doesn't have to be that way.

You should:
    Focus on the problem and not the blame.
    And try not to put anyone to shame.
    Don't yell or scream or put anyone down.
    Put a smile on your face and get rid of the frown.

(Chorus)

Look at the person who is talking to you
And show some respect for his opinions too!
Listen to suggestions and a different point of view.
And respect the feelings of other people too!

(Chorus)

Here's what you need to do
if someone is bothering you:

> *Work it out!*
> *Stop, Think, Listen and Talk*
> *And work it out*
> *Because it doesn't have to be that way.*

You need to :
    Fix the problem and not the blame
    Because this is really your major aim.
    Respect the feelings of other people too.
    Treat them the way —-you want them to treat you!

> *(Chorus)*

Don't let your pride get in the way
And keep you from saying what you need to say.
Take a look at the situation from the other person's view.
And say that **"I'm Sorry"** when it feels right for you!

> *(Chorus)*

> **Keep on talking** until you work out a solution. Then shake hands because you have **just succeeded in Conflict Resolution.**

Politics on the Plantation

Admiral Stern, the president, was another retired military man. He was very autocratic and none of his staff really liked him except for my boss because they were good friends. It's amazing how grown men act sometimes. In some of the meetings, I watched the snickering and the passing of notes while the president was talking. Obviously, he did not see this going on because none of these guys would have the guts to do or say these things to his face. The major complaint about *Admiral Stern* was that he was too rigid. It was his way or the highway.

My boss, *Phil Carefree*, was viewed by the staff as the *Admiral's* "Fair Haired Boy." Phil was a master politician who knew what to do to survive. He played a lot of golf and he had contacts with many people especially in the government arena. Basically, I got along with *Phil* although I did not have a lot of respect for him. And I definitely did not trust him. He was accustomed to people who would jump through hoops when he asked them to do so. That was not my style and I was not a "brown noser."

One of the other managers who worked for Phil was very comfortable doing whatever was asked of him. *John Gopher* was a skilled writer and he parlayed his skill together with his willingness to serve his boss to help him move ahead. Basically, there is nothing wrong with doing that if that is what you want to do. But invariably other people, including the people you are helping, lose a little respect for you as a person. It paid off for *John*, however, because he was promoted to director which was what he wanted.

In the corporate world, they rarely fire any executives. When they want to get rid of top executives they always "promote" them to another position. Oftentimes the position has less status and perks but it does allow the executive to "save face." *Admiral Stern* was moved to another position and a member of his staff was named to take his place. Ironically, his replacement was one of the people who used to complain about *Admiral Stern* behind his back. The new president, *Mr. Phony Liberal*, was a deceitful person. He made a name for himself in the government side of the business working with the Job Corps. He was "supposedly" committed to helping unemployed and under employed people. Everyone who laughs in your face and pats you on your back is not necessarily your friend. *Mr. Phony Liberal* did not like my boss so when he took over the presidency he told my boss, *Phil Carefree*, to find another job. My boss who always landed on his feet found another job in the Washington, D.C. area.

I was supposed to be my Boss' back-up and next in line for his position. But *Mr. Phony Liberal* had other plans. No way was he going to allow a Black man to become a vice-president. Here is a series of incredible events that happened. First, the new president decided *not* to replace *Phil Carefree*. He told me that I would report directly to him along with *John Gopher* who he promoted to director. He placed *John* in charge of the remaining people in the department. So I asked the new president why I was not considered for *Phil's* position and he told me that he decided that it did not need to be filled. So I along with *John* reported to the president for a short period of time.

Then one day a few months later during a staff meeting, the president, *Mr. Phony Liberal*, announced that a new Vice President of Strategic Planning was being hired from the outside and that I would be reporting to him. There was no warning at all. I learned about having a new boss along with everyone else. That was tacky and unprofessional. I just sat there, somewhat surprised, but I didn't say a word. No one else said anything either. They just looked at me as to say what are you going to do about it? Actually there was nothing I could do about it because it was the president's prerogative to pick whomever he desired for his staff.

All of the preparations were made for the arrival of the new VP. This included getting a nametag for his office, painting his name on his parking spot and the like. But a funny thing happened along the way. The candidate, for whatever reason, decided not to take the job. Now, Mr. *Phony Liberal* has egg on his face. After all of the hoopla what does he do now? I approached *Phony Liberal* and asked him if I would be considered for the position now, since he had decided to have a vice-president of Strategic Planning. I was certainly more than qualified for the position. He told me "no" and tried to explain to me that the person was being brought in from the outside due to special circumstances. He said that he was doing it as a favor for one of the corporate Vice Presidents. What a Crock! But any excuse will do because the bottom line was that he would not promote a Black to a vice president's position regardless of the situation. He actually looked me in my face and told me that bold face lie. There was nothing for me to do unless I wanted to leave the company. But I was not ready to leave yet.

A Female HNIC and the "Untouchables"

Operating the Job Corps facilities was a major contract for the Service Company. Since this was a government contract, the company hired more Blacks to work on the program. There was an attractive Black woman who was a Director on the Program. When I first joined the Service Company, I saw her in the cafeteria and we talked briefly. I did not know who she was or what position she held. So when she asked me if I had filled my opening for a secretary, I made the mistake of assuming that she was interested in applying for the job. As it turned out, she was going to recommend someone for the position. I was really embarrassed and I apologized to her but she was not offended by that mistake, she just did not ever let me forget about it.

Our relationship was strictly business and I would stop by her office from time to time to chat. But she would never open up to me and that bothered me for several reasons. As a man I found her very attractive. She was a classy lady who knew how to dress and how to carry herself in a business environment but she would always seem to be "up tight." I somewhat understood her plight because I saw in her the way I used to be when I first started to work in the corporate world some twenty years earlier.

It appeared that she wanted to be above reproach. I felt that she wanted to do a good job because she knew that she was in the spotlight. She was afraid to make a mistake or to be stereotyped as a woman and a Black who could not handle a key management position. Or even worse, she did not want to be viewed as a person who got a position simply because she was Black. I invited her to attend a Black Executive Exchange Program (BEEP) conference which was held in Atlanta each year. I thought that if she was around other Black executives, both males and females, that she would feel more comfortable. Even when she attended the BEEP Conference, she appeared to be uncomfortable and was reluctant to mingle with the others at the conference.

She was very close to her boss. I knew her boss and we would talk from time to time. He would brag to me about how he got her promoted to director and all the wonderful things he was doing for her. They traveled everywhere together on company business even overseas to places like Egypt. Of course, there were rumors that they had a thing going on but I certainly did not know anything. I was just hoping that they were false rumors. Only one thing made me a little suspicious. We were both nominated by RCA for the Harlem YMCA Black Achievers Award that was presented at a black tie affair at the New York Hilton in March 1985. This occurred one month after my wife had died of cancer.

After the affair was over, I was given an invitation to a reception in the penthouse of the hotel. I asked her if she received an invitation and when she said she had not, I asked her if she would like to go with me to the reception. She replied that she had something to do, and therefore declined. Later that evening, I saw her with her boss. Of course, she did not expect to see me because it was strictly by accident that I saw her. It did not necessarily mean anything because they were together but that was the first time I suspected something unusual might have been going on. I still remained cordial to her until I left the company. Later, I learned that she and her boss left the company to start their own business.

I had mixed emotions about a sister who might have been involved with her boss. Especially since he was married and she was a single parent trying to take care of her teenage kids. I knew she had a tough challenge trying to survive in the corporate world. So perhaps she had a mentor and maybe that was all her boss was to her. But I still maintain that you have to look at yourself in the mirror and if you like what you see then you're okay. But seeing her with him reminded me of something that I did not want to think about.

It reminded me of what Black women had to go through on the plantation as slaves. As a Black woman on the corporate plantation, she could not afford to be exploited by the White man as they had done to her ancestors. They raped them and did whatever they wanted to do, but the Black slave woman never got to sleep in the master's bedroom, in the big house, because that was reserved for the White lady of the house - his wife. It's okay to be a female HNIC as long as it is earned with your performance on the job.

It is usually accepted by Whites that a White man can talk to a Black woman at anytime regardless of his purpose. But when a Black man is seen talking to a White woman it sometimes causes problems. There has always been "night time" integration even on the plantation. We know about the masters taking advantage of slaves and even sometimes a frustrated White mistress forced the Black male slave to have sex with her. A Black man was living dangerously if he got caught having sex with a White woman. Oftentimes, if she was caught having sex with a Black, she would yell rape to cover the fact that she was the one who initiated the act. And the Black man was beaten, killed or lynched. We have seen theses incidents dramatized in movies like Roots and Mandingo. We have also read in books on how slaves were treated. During my time, I remember the story of a young Black boy, Emmett Till, who was killed because he allegedly whistled at a White woman. Although we see a lot of interracial dating and marriages today, things were a lot different in the 1960s.

There was an unwritten rule I followed. White women were off limits or taboo if you wanted to get ahead in the corporate environment. Many White women used to be afraid to talk to a Black man on or off the job for fear of being ostracized by their White coworkers. I know of a case where a brother was dating a White coworker and he was ultimately fired for a "sudden change in his performance" on the job. I am not suggesting that this type of harassment is blatant on the job today. Yet it still exists in more subtle ways. Nobody will say anything to a Black man who dates a White woman or is married to one today in most companies. Nevertheless, the attitudes are still present. The real acid test of a White male's friendship is to watch his reaction to you if you are flirting with or dating a White woman.

If he does not get upset and still remains friends with you then he basically passes that test and he can be considered a "regular guy." He is a person who can truly accept integration.

On the other hand, I know Blacks who don't like interracial marriages or interracial dating but many of these people are not in positions on the job to do anything about it. But what about the brother who comes to the company's party with a blond on his arm for all of world to see? How do you think those managers who might be bigots or racists will react when this brother is up for a promotion or raise? It happens all the time. A Black has to realize that he might be adding a liability if he decides to cross the line and date a White woman. I truly believe that a person should be able to date and marry whomever he or she wishes. But they must remember that they will have all of the problems a non-interracial couple has plus a host of new problems. It takes special people to make an interracial relationship work. My advice if you must do it, then go into it with your eyes open and be prepared to pay the price. Or you can do as I have done; consider White women as "untouchables."

Downsized

Some companies call it down sizing while others call it right sizing. But to me it is still a reduction of the work force or just an old fashion layoff. I have been the *"downsizer"* and the *"downsize"* and I don't like either one. In either case, it causes much stress and anxiety. As a manager, I hated having to make the decision that a certain number of the people reporting to me would lose their jobs. As more and more corporations move to cut expenses, they begin to downsize, right size or layoff employees. There used to be a time if you worked for IBM, Digital and many other Fortune 500 corporations, you had a job until you retired or until you decided you wanted to leave. But not anymore because the unwritten contract is broken. Company and employee loyalty is out of the window. Every person is for himself or herself. Some companies try to make it as painless as possible but it is still a very stressful situation for most people. This is especially true for people who had worked for the same company for twenty or more years.

During my career, I have been downsized three times. The first time I was able to find another job within two weeks of my notice. But in 1987, I was laid off from RCA after GE acquired the company. Everyone knew that there would be changes but no one expected the magnitude of changes that hit us. That by far was my worst experience. It was both frustrating and humiliating for me. Being separated from a job temporarily deprives you of a whole support system that most of us take for granted. I became angry because my downsizing was the result of an acquisition. The President of the newly formed company told us that *"talented people need not worry about their jobs."* He emphasized that employees from both RCA and GE would be given an equal opportunity at all open positions. But that was not what actually happened. Because I worked for the company that was acquired (RCA), no one even bothered to look at my resume or company records. Thousands of positions were eliminated without most of us being given an opportunity to compete for a position in the new company. It was like the saying, *"to the victor goes the spoils."*

Historically, when one company is acquired or merged with another, the company that is in the driver's seat typically sends in its henchmen to survey the spoils. They decide on what they are going to keep for themselves, what they are going to sell and what they are going to throw away. GE had a reputation of doing just that, especially its chairman, Jack Welch, who was nicknamed "Neutron Jack." It was said that his cuts were usually so severe that people compared his takeovers as being hit by a neutron bomb. They said he could wipe out an entire facility and leave only the walls and the roof standing.

Well all kinds of rumors were flying around the Service Company. So everyone got into a protective mode and tried to keep busy and keep their heads down. But you could not hide from reality. The GE management team swept through our division like an army on a rampage. They were like mercenaries raping the resources of a once proud company, rich in history and steeped in tradition. It was sad to witness plant closings. They took no prisoners, showed no mercy, and destroyed many dreams and careers. So I along with several hundred other employees including the president, *Mr. Phony Liberal*, were notified that we would be downsized. I was given about ninety days notice. That happened in 1987. From this experience, I learned how to vent my anger and to move on with my life. I was out of work for almost a year before I accepted a position with Digital Equipment Corporation. Since I had only been with the company for five years, I was not vested. In 1987, you had to be with the company ten years to be vested.

Although I did not think it would do much good, I decided to write a letter to the Chairman. I wanted to tell him how I felt about the way things were being handled. Here is the letter I wrote to the chairman.

(Letter to Chairman of GE.)

9999 E. Sedgwick Street
Philadelphia, Pa. 19150

October 2, 1986

Mr. John F. Welch, Jr.
Chairman and CEO
General Electric Corporation
3135 Easton Turnpike
Fairfield, CT. 06431

Dear Mr. Welch:

I was probably one of the few RCA employees who looked favorably upon the merger of RCA and GE. When I first heard about it, I felt that perhaps there would be more opportunities for me to advance. Despite all of the nice words said about the need for talented people, I soon learned that the welfare of an employee is the least concern of GE and RCA.

I have been given until the end of the year to find another position and I am optimistic that I will find one. My major disappointment is that no one from GE looked at my resume or Personal Data Summary Sheet. Although I was told that my layoff was due to the merger, I do not feel that GE alone is totally at fault.

Everyone tells me that I am a bright and talented person but there must not be opportunities for talented people in GE. I have a diversified background with considerable experience *in working with all levels of management, including the chief executive officers of several major corporations. I also have the ability to absorb highly complex information and communicate this information in simple terms as demonstrated by the ten books on computers I have written and published. For these reasons, and others, I have a problem rationalizing why there is no opportunity for me in GE.*

Since no one from GE looked at my resume (at least as of today), I am sending a copy of it to you so that you can see the kind of people GE is discarding without even checking their qualifications. I am not sending you my resume to seek reinstatement with GE because I have concluded that it is best for me to leave now. But I hope this letter will cause you to review your procedures for layoffs before you do more irreparable harm to quality people.

I regret having to write to you about this matter but it is important to me that I express my feelings. It is my opinion that GE will end up the biggest loser because if you do not treat your employees fairly, it will hurt you in the long run. As a former Director at RCA, I expected better treatment than I received.

Disappointed,

Aubrey B. Jones, Jr.

After I sent the letter, there was a flurry of activity by Employee Relations to cover up their ineptness. I received a CYA (Cover Your A_ _) memo from the RCA Service Company Division Vice President of Employee Relations. This memo was sent after I had a brief meeting with him to discuss the letter I had sent to the chairman. He obviously did not like what I had done and he told me so. He tried to refute my statement that my resume was not sent to anyone for review. But he assured me in his memo that they would continue to take all the appropriate action to communicate my qualifications throughout GE and RCA.

Cutting expenses by cutting people does not take much imagination. It is the easy way however for most corporations. It takes innovation, creativity, good planning and time to come up with alternatives. Most companies are not willing to invest the time to do this because time is money to them. I thought that GE might be different in its merger and would breathe new life into RCA which needed resuscitation. But I was wrong; GE sucked the blood out of RCA and destroyed a company that had much to offer if managed properly.

When a company is being downsized, affirmative action and EEO policies are ineffective. It is every person for himself or herself. Some companies will set up review procedures called a disparate review to determine if too many people of a certain class are being downsized. However, these procedures are usually put in place primarily to protect the company from class action suits and not to help the employee. My attitude has always been that I will never leave a company with my head between my legs. There are a lot more important things in life than a job. For those people who need a job to make themselves feel important, I pity them. One day they will wake up and life will have passed them by. They will have missed out on those things that are really important: Family, friends and happiness. On January 2, 1987, I was terminated officially from RCA. I was given a small severance package and free out-placement service. The president, *"Mr. Phoney Liberal,"* I was told received a "Golden Parachute" which meant that he was taken care of, just like many of the top executives in corporations after mergers.

Keep a *Positive Attitude!*

Positive attitudes create positive energy
and
Positive energy helps you *Get the Job You Want*

A Sobering Experience

One of the most humiliating things for me was to have to go to the unemployment office in Camden, New Jersey. I debated whether or not to even collect unemployment because I had saved some money, and financially, I would be okay for a while. Nevertheless, I decided to collect unemployment, but standing in those long snaking lines was embarrassing and dehumanizing. They treated you like you were a nobody. The clerks were very cold and discourteous. All kinds of people were in line. After a while I became immune to the way that I was treated and just did what I had to do and got out as fast as I could. In 1987, my son, Aubrey III, was in college and my daughter, Adrienne, was in high school. Although my daughter was old enough to take care of herself, I did not like leaving her at home by herself for long periods of time. One of the reasons I did not want to relocate was because I had a support system for my daughter in the neighborhood. Her best friend's mother, Chris Meadows, was a surrogate mother for Adrienne. This was really a big help to me after my wife died.

Being out of work impacts you in other ways too. In 1987, when I told people that I was downsized, some of them acted as though there was something wrong with me. I learned who my real friends were. The most frustrating thing was that many people would not return my telephone calls. I found that a few people who I had helped in the past and thought of as friends were not available. They acted as if they had forgotten me and avoided me at all costs. Perhaps they assumed I was going to ask them for a job. Although it hurt, I had to move on and dismiss their behavior as simple apathy or living with fear of their own insecurity. When I went out to a party or any other social event and met people, invariably they would ask me "What are you doing these days?" And when I would say: "I'm out of work or I was downsized," they usually didn't know what to say. Some people thought that I had a lot more money than I did because of the success with my books. Others probably thought that I was not working by choice or perhaps I had retired. They just could not understand how I could be out of a job, and neither could I!

Choices Power Dreams

Thinking **Big!**

"You Have the Power to Choose
What You Want to Do"

Finding a Job on Another Plantation

Finding a job is a full time job. I did not think it would take me as long as it did to find a new job. It took me well over a year to find a job in 1987 because I was not willing to relocate my family. Initially, I was reluctant to use the out-placement services because I did not think it would be worth my time to use these services since I knew how to write my resume. But to my surprise, there were some benefits to using Right Associates outplacement services. First of all, they provided me with an office so that I could make telephone calls anywhere I wanted to. They also provided support services like typing, resume writing and career counseling if needed. An out placement service will not find a job for you, but they will teach you how find yourself a job.

To do an effective job search, you have to prepare a personal marketing campaign. It is analogous to a product marketing campaign. To successfully market a product, you must identify the product characteristics, package it properly, and promote it to potential customers. Out-placement services teach you how to network. They remind you that most of the available positions are not advertised in newspapers or employment agencies. To find out where the jobs are, you have to network into companies that might have opportunities for you. One of the things I learned about networking was the informational interview. This is where you meet with someone in a company that you have targeted to find out more about that industry or whatever additional information you might need. But what you are really doing is building your network because at a minimum you want that person to give you the name of someone else you can talk to. If you do this enough times, it should eventually lead to a job interview. It works, but it takes patience and perseverance.

It is very frustrating at times trying to find a job because people will not always return your phone calls. You also might answer hundreds of want ads and contact many search firms with no luck. So you have to be patient, and that was a very difficult thing for me because patience is not one of my virtues. What I learned is that people will try to exploit you if they think that you are anxious to find work. I remember networking into a software distributor and I had a very good meeting with the president. So he asked me to come back to meet with his senior vice president of marketing. In preparation for my meeting, I prepared a proposal on how I could add value to their company. After the VP marketing and I talked for a while, he asked me, "how much did you need to live on?" I told him that I had not really thought about it. What he was really asking me is "what is the minimum salary we can hire you for." That approach turned me off and I did not pursue it any more. Initially, I would have liked to work for the company, but his approach told me that he was not the kind of person I wanted to work with. I also worked as an independent consultant for a small minority firm who wanted to hire me as a general manager but was having a cash flow problem and could not afford me.

One of the most disappointing experiences I had while networking was with a brother at Bell of Pennsylvania. I was given his name by several people as the person to talk to at Bell. He was truly the HNIC. After writing him a letter and calling many times, he finally agreed to meet with me. Although I should have known better, but I thought that my reception would have been different since I was meeting with a brother. After all, this was the HNIC who had the power to help out another brother. But I forgot that there can be only one HNIC per plantation and if you are the HNIC, you don't want anyone else around who could possibly replace you. This brother looked at my resume and said, *"If you can do all these things, why do you need to work here?"* Needless to say I got no support there. So I thanked him for his time and left.

I found my next job by attending a job fair sponsored by Digital Equipment Corporation. I knew that my qualifications did not match the type of people they were looking for, but I went to the job fair with the intention of networking into the company. And it worked. However, it was about five months later before I actually was offered a job as a Sales Support

Manager at Digital Equipment Corporation's Mount Laurel, New Jersey office. I started with digital on December 21, 1987 almost one year from my official termination date from RCA.

For interviews, remember to:

Be Prepared

Act like you are Confident

Look like you are Confident

Be Confident, but not Overly-Confident

IX. Life on an "Un-Managed" Plantation-DEC

A Rough Start

I started at Digital just before the Christmas holidays began. It was my choice on when I could start and I was anxious to get started as soon as possible. One advantage of starting during the holiday season was that many of the employees took vacation time along with the holidays. This was a perfect time to come in to read policies and procedures, learn how to use the computer systems and set my priorities for the coming year. Working at Digital was a totally unique experience. Although I had over twenty years experience as a manager in other corporations, I was not prepared for Digital. One of the reasons Digital had to go outside for managers was because the company was growing so fast that they did not have enough qualified internal candidates. A question everyone would ask me was, "What do you think about Digital?" And then they would smile and wait for my response. I would usually say that Digital had *"Good People, Good Products, Poor Management and No Marketing!"* Basically, no one disagreed with me.

My first few months were a challenge for me. My boss was a very bright analytical type manager who had very poor people skills. He was much more comfortable in one-on-one meetings than in group meetings. His style of management could be best categorized as "management by conflict." He felt that if things were very quiet in the units then the managers were not doing their jobs. As a District Manager, he had about a dozen direct reports. There were two Sales Support Managers, *Diane Friendly* and myself. *Diane* was hired from the outside also, about five months earlier than I. Now *Diane* and I did not hit it off real well in the beginning primarily because we had two different styles of management. Her style was more amicable with her direct reports and she got very close to them. She would get involved in their personal as well as business issues. She was more of a nurturing "mother hen" type with her people. In contrast, I was more of a director type manager in that I would try to make certain that everyone knew what had to be done and I expected them to do it. I treated everyone as a professional until they proved that they were not.

Another reason I had some problems was that my boss told his staff that he was bringing in a very experienced manager who will help straighten up this place. I did not find this out until about six years later when I was talking to *Ron Angry* who had told people he did not like me. I asked him why he did not like me. He said that when I came on board he thought that I was an arrogant SOB because I said that "I was going to straighten this place out." I did not remember saying those words but I did not deny that I might have. After all, that was one of the reasons I thought I was hired, and perhaps my boss had said this to a few people also.

When I came on board, *Diane* and the other managers were probably a little leery of me because of expectations that were set by my boss. For example, I got resistance when I made a suggestion that we survey the skills of the technical people in both units so that we would know their capabilities and who needed training. *Diane* told her unit that they did not have to provide this information unless they wanted to do so. I had all the people in my unit fill out the survey so that I could use it as an example of how it would look. It did not help the cause when my boss thought it was a good idea. I heard *Diane* say, "I have good ideas too!" Word was getting around the office that *Diane* and I did not like each other and that our units would not work together. For the most part, the perceptions were accurate. This was bad for morale and my boss just kept telling us that we had to work it out.

Because of the problems Diane and I had working together, someone from employee relations got involved. I will call her *Ms. Tattle Tale* because she was known to spread rumors even when things were told to her in the strictest confidence. She asked to meet with me to discuss my relationship with *Diane*. When I met with her, she told me that *Diane* was saying some "scandalous" things about me to everyone. Although she did not elaborate, she did say that *Diane* told her that "I did not know how to manage Sales Support." I told *Ms Tattle Tale* that I do not participate in petty gossip and that I would not stoop to that level of mud slinging even though it was happening to me. She asked if I would participate in a meeting with *Diane*. I asked for what purpose. She said so that we could air things out. I told her that I had tried before and that I did not trust *Diane* because she talks negatively about everyone, including her boss and even about *Ms. Tattle Tale*. I would not have felt comfortable talking to *Diane* with *Ms. Tattle Tale* as the moderator because I did not think she was capable of handling the situation. Nor did I think our discussions would be held in confidence.

This conflict between Diane and me continued for a while, so I prayed about it because it was really starting to affect my performance on the job. *Diane* and I had to work together to be successful. So I went to work the next day not knowing what I was really going to do but I was confident that I would do the right thing. So I asked *Diane* to stop by my office so we could talk. The first thing that I told her was that *"I was not the enemy and that I was on her side."* Further, I told her that I would help her before I would hurt her. Her response was that she felt I was trying to tell her how to do her job. She told me that although she might not have as much experience as I had, she was still a good manager with good skills. Then she began to tell me how she felt about our boss. She did not trust him at all and was very outspoken about how she felt about him to anyone who would listen. She even told him to his face how she felt about him. She was so paranoid about him that she would not go into his office by herself. Ironically, I became her confidant and her support. When she had to meet with our boss, she always wanted me to be present.

Things began to get better after *Diane* and I started to work together. We held joint unit meetings and supported each other's effort. Our boss never wanted to believe that *Diane* and I had worked things out. He did not think that it was possible. *Diane*, however, made a tactical and political mistake by openly bad mouthing our boss. I did not like his management style either but my rule was very simple. If I work for you, I will support you because I expected the same from people who reported to me. As it turned out, *Diane* was moved out of Sales Support to another position which she did not like but she accepted it anyhow. She still reported to the same person, however, but in a different capacity. In the long term, this was good for her because it gave her some experience in another area but it did not do anything for her relationship with our boss. *Diane* and I still remained friends after both of us left Digital.

Skip a Level Meetings

Although I had worked for a number of different companies, I had never heard of *skip a level meeting*. This is a meeting where the people who report to you meet with your boss without you being present. It was intended to provide an open channel of communications for the employees to the next higher level of management without fear of reprisals from their manager. Depending on how the meeting was handled, it could provide some very constructive feedback. But oftentimes these meetings became bitching sessions. It is up to the person moderating the session to not let it deteriorate into a negative meeting. Needless to say, I was crucified at the first meeting according to the written feedback I received from my boss. Digital employees were very independent and they were not used to anyone giving them direction. Individuals who are used to governing themselves usually have different ideas about how to solve problems. As a result, this causes conflict and to resolve conflicts required timely negotiating.

For example, there were times when a sales rep needed support. If the sales support specialist did not want to assist the sales rep, for whatever reason, the specialist would just say he was busy. The specialists kept their own schedules and did not like giving their schedules to the unit's secretary. To them, that was micro-managing. When we tried to institute a sign out log and a weekly calendar, many of the specialists refused to enter the information. In fact, it was even difficult to get them to report their weekly times on the computerized system set up to capture the data. In a nutshell, there was no discipline. So when I came on board trying to bring some discipline to the organization, everybody started to complain except my boss. He knew it was needed and he did support my efforts.

When my boss sent me a copy of the results of the *skip a level* meeting, he sent me a note "to thicken my skin." He said that I would need thick skin to digest the feedback objectively. Most of the feedback was not unexpected. Both units expressed concerns over the like of harmony between the two units. One comment was: *"We are people caught in the middle of a battle between the two unit managers (Speaking about Diane and me)."* They went on to complain about my management style and indicated that I always sided with sales reps and did not defend them. They said my feedback was normally couched with, "When I was at CDC...RCA...we did it this way." According to the feedback, they did not want to hear about how I worked in the past. They said, "I was off base when trying to give directions to the specialists on how to do their jobs" (Even though I was their manager!). They went on and on, and the report was two and a half pages of bulleted line items. After thinking about the report for a while, I realized that I must have been doing something right because most people tend to resist change. I was not there to win a popularity contest but to get the job done the best way I knew how.

Important Lesson Learned
Even When You Know or Think That You're Right, Be Patient!
Patience is a Virtue!
It's a Beneficial Quality or Power
It's a Commendable Quality or Trait
It's a Must for Good Leadership and Team Building.

Handling Prima Donnas

Perhaps one thing that I did that demonstrated to the employees that I had their best interest in mind was to support the promotion of a sales support specialist. The specialist name was *Saul* who was frustrated in his attempts to get promoted. When I had to give him his first performance review, it was not a very good one. Because I was not his manager for the full period of his performance, I had to rely on feedback from his previous manager. *Saul* told me that it was not fair for me to review him because I had not known him long enough. I told *Saul* that if he wanted to get promoted there were some things he had to do first. One of the things that he had to do was to get some training on Digital Workstations.

After talking to *Saul* for a while, I learned why he was so bitter and resistant to being trained on these workstations. At one time, he was a support specialist for Digital's unsuccessful Rainbow product line which was Digital's first entry into the PC market. Due to poor sales of the product, the company dropped it. This action left a bad taste in the mouths of the people who supported it. *Saul* viewed the workstation product line as similar to the Rainbow, a loser, and he wanted no part of it. I told *Saul* that we needed additional support on this new product and if he agreed to do this I would support a promotion for him. He agreed to give it a try. When *Saul* left my office, he thanked me for being honest with him and for my support.

To get a promotion in Sales Support at the Mount Laurel Office was like nothing I had ever heard of before. Supposedly, for a specialist to get promoted, he or she had to have the support of his or her manager together with the support of another manager and a technical consultant. The specialist's manager was responsible for writing up a recommendation for promotion and presenting it at the staff meeting for approval. If the specialist was very popular, it was easy for an approval. But if a specialist had stepped on someone's toes along the way, the promotion could be held up indefinitely. *Saul* thought that the reason he did not get promoted was because he did not have the needed support of consultants. But upon further investigation, I learned that none of his previous managers had ever supported his promotion **but they never told him so**. Or if they told him, he did not hear them because he thought he always had the support of his manager.

After *Saul* completed his training and accomplished most of the things on his goal sheet, I proceeded to start the promotion process for him. *Diane*, the other Sales Support Manager, said she would support *Saul* and I had the support of three technical consultants so I assumed that it was a done deal. **Wrong**! As it turned out my boss did not think *Saul* was ready for promotion and challenged my support. We went around and around on this one. My boss asked for each of the people who was supporting *Saul* to put it in writing. This was highly unusual because normally he would just ask for verbal support in a staff meeting. For some unknown reason, my boss did not want *Saul* promoted so he put a lot of "pain and suffering" in the process to try to discourage his supporters. Most of the other managers knew that our boss did not like *Saul* but I would not back down. *Saul* was overdue for a promotion and I felt that he had been treated unfairly. In the end, my boss gave in and *Saul* was promoted. Word got around on how I fought for *Saul's* promotion and for once the specialist knew that I was a man of my word. They learned that if I made a commitment to you, then you could bank on it, unless something happened totally out of my control.

As I mentioned earlier, many of Digital employees were very independent. If they did not want to do something they did not do it. This was especially true of many of the technical specialists who thought that they were indispensable. Many felt that as long as they remained technical they did not have to worry about other skills. Some of them lacked interpersonal, communications and administrative skills. I watched other managers and sales reps beg and cajole sales support specialists to take on assignments - assignments which were part of their job responsibilities. I remember *Al*, a networks guru, who had a number of idiosyncrasies. For example, he was very comfortable doing one-on-one presentations but he hated to stand before a group of people to explain anything. I believe that he was a Liberals Arts major in college and he was proud of the fact that most of his technical knowledge was picked up on his own. Basically, I did not have a problem with him until he walked in my office and cursed at me.

I do not remember all of the events that led up to this incident but I think this story illustrates what I had to put up with when trying to manage Prima Donnas. As I recall, *Al* wanted a transfer to another department or to someplace he could get more hands on experience. He said he needed to keep abreast with the changing technology. At the time, it was not possible for him to do that, so before we could finish our conversation, he stood up and said, "I don't need to take this sh__ plus some other expletives deletives." Then, he walked out of my office slamming the door behind him. Well, the next day my boss called me in and asked me what happened. After I told him, he said that I needed to talk to *Al* again. But my attitude was that *Al* needed to talk to Human Resources because I was not going to tolerate that kind of behavior. It was unprofessional and unneeded. My boss pleaded *Al's* case pointing out how good a technical person he was and that he wanted me to talk to *Al* again. So I reluctantly agreed to do so.

When *Al* came into my office to meet with me, I could tell he was very nervous because "he knew he had shot himself in the foot." I was cool. I asked *Al* why he cursed at me because I certainly did not remember doing anything to provoke that type of behavior. Then I got a shock. A true confession for the first time from a White man. First he started crying. Then he told me that I intimidated him. He said that he had never dealt with a Black man like me before. *Al* admitted that he was a very insecure person who was not real sure what he wanted to do. He said that he perceived me as being a strong person and had a hard time dealing with me. Further, he told me that he started out as a musician in the Chicago area and his only contact with Blacks was through music until he met me. He went on to say that he was an only child who was now taking care of his sickly mother.

Initially, I did not know what to say or do. He had such a sob story that he almost made me want to cry. Was this a scam by a con artist trying to overcome a mistake that he had made and now was fighting for his job? I didn't know for sure but I gave him the benefit of the doubt. I agreed to help him get more hands on experience. In fact, I arranged to let him work at our nearby technology center two days a week to help him stay abreast of the latest technology. When he left the meeting, I thought we had a workable agreement. But a few months later, he requested a transfer to another department where he took on a long-term assignment at a customer's site. He left my unit for a year and then he came back to Sales Support, but this time he reported to a different manager. Perhaps that was what he wanted to do all along.

The "Matrix-Managed" Plantation

The best way I can describe the "matrix-managed" organization at Digital is to call it an "Unmanaged" plantation. In a typical field office, there were four District Managers (DM), one for each of the major functions. There was a Sales DM, Software Services DM, Operations DM and a Maintenance Services DM. Each organization had its own goals and measurements for success which were sometimes conflicting. If there was a dispute between Sales and Software Services, theoretically, the two DMs were supposed to get together and resolve their dispute. It rarely happened that way especially if the two heads of the departments did not like one another or if the decision in some way conflicted with the goals of the other department.

Here is a typical situation that occurred a number of times. Sales were measured on Certifications or bookings of new business but Software Services were measured on Billings and Revenue. If sales had the opportunity for a large sale of a computer system and the customer needed support from Software Services, oftentimes sales would try to give away that services at cost so that they could keep the price down and make the sale. Whereas, it might be good for the corporation to make the sale, it does not help the Software Services DM to make his numbers and he comes out on the short end of the stick. But on the other hand, the Sales DM looks like a hero and he would get the bonus at the end of the year.

In my opinion, inconsistent goals for separate organizations were one of the major reasons for the decline of Digital. We made the sale but the profit margin was minimal in some cases. For example, Digital sold millions of dollars worth of computers to Dupont Corporation, but the level of support that was provided severely impacted the profit margin. It took Digital a number of years to realize that they could not continue to do business that way. But it was too late to change and downsizing was inevitable.

Ken Olsen, the founder and President of Digital, was a brilliant and very jovial person. He loved technology and tolerated marketing although he did not like it. He embraced the matrix-management system. He loved the competitiveness it caused among departments. This works well for a research and design environment but not for customer service. As one of our customers who was addressing a Digital's dinner put it, "I want one fanny on the line; I do not want to have to talk to ten different people to get resolution to my problem."

The Digital matrix management system has been studied,

written about and laughed at by many people. There was even an internal video made for sales on how Digital responded to customer requests. It showed a customer with a very simple problem and how Digital paraded a large number of people in front of him before he was able to get to the right person with his solution. Most people who saw the video laughed and most Digital employees accepted the system as a way of life. It was very difficult to get a decision in Digital because you had to get consensus and buy-in from everyone before a decision could be made.

I was criticized on my first performance review for making "too many quick decisions." So I asked my boss "how many of the decisions were right decisions" and if I was making quick wrong decisions then he would have a valid complaint. I think what he was trying to tell me (although he did not explain it this way) that although my decisions might have been right, I did not give the others time enough to buy into my decisions. This was the way things were done at Digital. It was different and new for me so I had to make some adjustments to my management style.

Although I was a first-line manager at Digital, I felt like a first line administrator. We had very little freedom to make decisions that are usually made routinely at other companies. Decisions such as who gets promoted, who gets a raise and how much of a raise you can give someone. Digital used a company wide computerized salary management system. It was a great tool to help manage the process. But it limited the manager's flexibility on how you rewarded your people. The system was based on the principle that you pay for performance. The higher your performance the higher your reward. At Digital, it was the first time that I sat in a room with all of the other managers and a representative from Human Resources to determine who will get a raise and how much in the next year. As managers, we were required to forecast the next year's performance rating for the people reporting to us. And based on this rating, we would rank our direct reports with other employees in the district and the highest ranked employees would get an increase.

I don't have a problem with setting guidelines for promotions and increases, but the manager should be allowed to make the decision for his unit on who gets an increase. It should not be done by a committee. Apparently, Digital did not have enough confidence in its managers that we would make the right decisions so everything was controlled by the corporate system. I would have preferred to have a pool of money allocated for my unit and then let me determine the best way to distribute using corporate guidelines. One of the guidelines that really bothered me, and most of the other managers, was that only a certain percentage of the people could get a raise in a single year regardless of their performance. This is analogous to being a teacher and telling your class that only 60% of you would pass even if you all worked very hard and passed all of the tests.

There was another event that caused much stress, anxiety and frustration. It was the annual selection of who would win the "Circle of Excellence" award. This was the grand prize that all of the field employees wanted to win. It was an all expensed paid trip for the employee and significant other to go to places like Hawaii, or Australia for about a week. It was a great experience if you had the opportunity to attend. The only problem was there were only a limited number of slots available usually less than 10% of the total number of employees could participate. In order to make the selection, we would have a staff meeting and each manager would come in with his or her nominees' names and the supporting documentation. Each person was ranked and then voted on by the group. Sounds like a democratic way to do it but it wasn't.

There was intense lobbying to get support for certain employees. Those employees with the most visibility had an easier time of gaining support. Oftentimes it was the senior level employees who won the trip. But these meetings could get real ugly pitting manager against manager. Each manager trying to fight for his or her subordinates so that they would be in a better position to win the trip. Additionally, even if a person won, he or she could not share the good news with other employees. That's because sometimes there was jealousy and animosity toward the winners. Only those people who were clear winners because their performance was head and shoulders above the rest could celebrate. Some employees would lobby their mangers and would threaten to quit if they did not win. Circle of Excellence was supposed to be a motivation and a morale booster for the employees. Unfortunately, it usually only demoralized those who did not win especially those employees who thought they should have won.

Leadership

Leadership is an influence process
That helps insure other people's success

Leadership is knowing that other people
are influenced by you
But recognizing that they in turn influence you too

Leadership is setting goals so people will know
Which way you want them to go

Leadership is organizing the people
and communicating the needs
While energizing them through words and deeds

Leadership is getting people to perform well
And doing it without a hard sell

Leadership is accepting a new idea from someone
But actively encouraging new ideas from everyone

Leadership is making people feel important to you
And convincing them that their work is important too

Leadership is inspiring confidence in someone
By showing confidence in everyone

Leadership is getting the job done
And making everyone feel like they've won

The Blue Bell Plantation

I lived in Philadelphia and the Mount Laurel office was approximately 25 miles from my house. To get to work, it would take me 45 minutes to an hour one way depending on the traffic. So when there was an opening for the same position at Digital's Blue Bell, Pennsylvania office, I applied for it. This office was only five miles from where I lived and it only took me 15-20 minutes to get to work.

Blue Bell was a different Sales District which covered a different territory than the district in New Jersey. They were having all kinds of problems in Blue Bell especially with Sales Support. Further, it was perceived to be a racist environment in this office. One of the vice presidents in Software Services told me that he was happy to see me go to Blue Bell for a number of reasons. He believed I would be able to help organize sales support and integrate the office because, for some reason Blacks, were not hired there. The official reason given why there were no Blacks in that office was because it was in the suburbs and it was not close to public transportation. But transportation was not an issue because Black professionals had cars.

In Digital's matrix-management structure, the Sales Support Manager reported to two DMs. A solid line reporting to the Software Services DM and a dotted line reporting to the Sales DM. So I had my first interview with the Software Services DM, *Ron Easyrider*, which went extremely well. Then I had to meet with the Sales DM, *Herb Hickman*, who did not want me to come to Blue Bell. But *Herb* and *Ron* never agreed on many things anyway, and in this case *Ron* was actually the hiring manager. I found out later that *Herb*, who was from West Virginia, had some preconceived notions about Black people. After *Herb* got to know me better, he changed his opinion of me. In fact, he told me at my first performance review that he was glad *Ron* had the good sense to hire me.

So that I would not make the same mistakes that I made when I came on board at the Mount Laurel office, I met with my counterpart, *Carol Slick*. I did this before it was announced that I was moving to the Blue Bell office. I wanted to learn what she thought the problems were at Blue Bell for sales support. She acknowledged that she had problems with the former sales support manager who left the company. She explained that there were two sales support units but they were not permitted to work together. It was much worse than what I had experienced at Mount Laurel. So we talked about how we would work together to improve the morale and effectiveness of sales support. One of the first things we did was to have a joint unit meeting to introduce me to all of the sales support specialists.

My secretary, *Mary Jayne Brown*, was Black and had been with Digital for sometime. She filled me in with the inside scoop on everybody. *Mary Jayne* warned me to watch my back because she had encountered some problems of her own. She was a large Black woman, who was very outspoken, and although some of the people did not like her nobody messed with *Mary Jayne*. She worked as my secretary only for a few months before she left the company on a disability.

Within the first month I had two resignations from my unit. Everyone made a joke about it because they said my reputation had preceded me. But as it turned out these people were already looking for new jobs before I moved to Blue Bell. With the two resignations and with some new open requisitions, I had the opportunity to hire some new people. One of my goals was to hire some qualified minorities for the office. I had met a couple of Blacks who worked in different offices who had expressed an interest in coming to Blue Bell. Both of these people had applied for positions there before but were not hired.

Robert Jenkins started working for Digital in the Field Service Department, later he transferred to Software Services in the Delaware office. As a software services specialist, he had varied assignments at customer sites. He did not like the kind of work he was doing because he felt he was in a dead end job. He wanted out of the delivery side of Software Services. When I first met with Rob, he told me that he wanted to go into management because he felt that he would have a better chance for advancement. My recommendation to him was to stay technical for now because there was a lot more security as a technical person. Because of his background and experience, I suggested that he try sales support. In sales support, he would get a lot of visibility and he would learn a lot. Rob told me that he had applied for a position in sales support at Blue Bell a year ago but he was turned down because he was told he did not have enough experience.

When I called his manager to get permission to interview him and to ask for his records, I learned that he had been put on probation. At Digital, they call it being put on a development plan. So I asked his manager, why he was put on probation and she said, "He doesn't seem to have the analytical skills needed to do the job!" I said to her "Help me to understand something. Here is a man who has two college degrees, one of which is in Computer Science where he finished with a 3.5 average and he doesn't have analytical skills?" And I continued, "Could it be that he just does not like his job?" She said, "Come to think of it, he did say he did not like programming." Duh! He was placed in the wrong assignment and nobody bothered to do anything about it except write him up as a poor performer. I could not believe what I was hearing but I knew his manager and she did not have a good track record as a manager.

After I learned that Rob was on probation, I did not tell anyone in sales support because I knew he would do an outstanding job. Further, I did not want the other sales support manager, who had to interview him, to use the probation as an excuse for not hiring him. He had all the skills that we were looking for in specialists. All he needed was some additional training on the products and an opportunity to demonstrate his talents. So Rob was hired. He had been neglected by management and he was way below where he should have been in level and salary range. One of my priorities was to get him to his proper salary level.

In Digital, if your manager did not look out for you, nobody else would do it. Rob turned out to be an outstanding sales support specialist as I had expected. In sales support, he was like a new person and he liked what he was doing. I have learned that your job as an employee is to make your manager look good by doing good work and a **good** manager, in turn, will look out for you.

I told the story of Rob because it is hard to prove whether or not he was neglected because he was Black or because his manager was just a poor manager or both. But if I had made an issue of why he was not hired, there would have been all kinds of excuses made. Sometimes racism is right in front of people but they will deny that it exists. Although racism exists on the corporate plantations, it is usually not blatant. As a Black man, I accepted the fact that racism was present but I did not let it stop me from doing my job. As I mentioned earlier in this book, one of the things I used to test for racism was the checklist approach.

When a situation occurs that I suspect it might be because of racism, I try to keep an open mind and evaluate what happened. I want to make certain that I am not overreacting. I try to look at it from the other person's perspective and I consider the source. In the end, if I rule out everything else then the only thing I can say is, "Maybe So" but I know I could never prove it. As long as I am not in any physical danger, I learned never to respond to a remark or an incident. I just "keep getting up" (i.e. moving on) as the brothers say. Sometimes I might even smile at the person but it would be a mistake to assume that my smile is a sign of weakness. On the contrary, it is a sign of strength - An inner strength that helps me to rise above a negative situation because no human can bring me down unless I allow him to do so.

We made some progress in recruiting Blacks to Blue Bell. Marcia Henderson was the next minority that I help recruit for Blue Bell. I met Marcia in 1983 because at that time she was teaching word processing for Digital. I was not working for Digital then but I purchased a Digital word processing system so that my wife could type my manuscripts for my computer books. So my wife took a one-day course on word processing and Marcia was her instructor. When I was hired by Digital in 1987, Marcia called me because she was interested in moving to sales support. I met with her and told her that she did not have the skills for sales support at that time but gave her a list of things that I felt she needed to do to qualify for a job in sales support. When I moved to Blue Bell, I contacted Marcia and told her that we had an opening that she might qualify for. But I told her to sell herself to *Carol Slick* first because she already had my support. The reason I told her to go to *Carol* first was because *Carol* had rejected her before and I wanted *Carol's* support for my hiring Marcia. She was hired.

So now there were three Blacks specialists in Sales Support, Michael Jackson who was hired by *Carol Slick* just before I came to Blue Bell, Rob Jenkins and Marcia Henderson. Just for the record, I hired other specialists who were not Black during that same period. But since the previous management said that it was having a difficult time hiring minorities, I made it one of my priorities. I helped recruit another Black lady who relocated from Massachusetts, Debra Claussen who actually reported to *Carol Slick* to provide some balance between the two units. After all the effort to recruit minorities, we lost two during the first downsizing. Debra Claussen was going to leave anyway because she got married and was moving to California and Marcia Henderson, who by the guidelines that were established for downsizing, was on the bubble.

"Black Notes"-The Communications Network

Digital was one of the first companies that I worked for that had a company-wide electronics communications network (E-Mail) for all employees. This was a very effective system of sending mail and messages to anyone on the network. It is not uncommon today to see many other companies with E-Mail but I would have to believe Digital was one of the leaders. As a high tech company, Digital used its networks for more than just E-Mail. It was possible to access databases with all kinds of technical information.

There was also the very popular notes file. "Notes," as it was called internally, allowed subscribers to tap into the system and find out information on almost any topics (Very similar to "chat rooms" on the Internet today). Initially, the "Notes" file was used for technical information. For example, if you were a software specialist and was having a problem with a particular application or product, you could search the notes file to see if anyone had started a conference on that subject. Starting a conference simply meant that someone had set up space for a file on a disk and gave it a name. A notes session could be started with a simple question like, "Has anyone had a problem with loading or debugging a specific application?" Then subscribers to the notes conference would start a discussion about their experiences with the problem and what they did to resolve it and so on. As I said, you could start a notes conference on any topic. So some Blacks within Digital started a conference on Black issues called *"Black Notes."*

Black Notes reminded me of how the slaves communicated from plantation to plantation. They called it night walks. After sundown and the slaves had finished working the in the fields for the day, they would sneak to other nearby plantations under the cover of darkness to see loved ones and friends to let them know what was going on. They could also use these night walks to meet and plan escapes from the plantation. Since subscribers to the notes files did not have to use their real names, they could remain anonymous and not have to fear reprisals if someone did not like what they wrote to the file. Similarly, slaves on the plantation had codes that they would use to communicate to one another. Oftentimes the code was communicated through singing spirituals and work songs while they were on the plantation picking cotton or doing whatever they had to do as a slave. Some of the topics of the notes files included: "Tale of Black Notes," "Black People United," "Promotions and Mentors" "O.J. Simpson" and "Denny's Restaurant." The topics could be on anything of interest to Black people. There were subscribers who had a problem even calling it Black Notes instead of "African-American" notes. Black Notes was a way for the Black employees to express their frustration with Digital and other plantations. It was a good way to speak out and let off some steam.

A Real HNIC

At one time, Digital was a good place for Black Employees. It was written up in a number of articles on how Digital was a model corporation for managing diversity. But when hard times beset a company, most companies start cutting back on social responsibilities and everyone gets into the protective mode. There were several real HNICs at Digital. By real HNICs, I mean high level executives with profit and loss responsibilities and the power to make or impact major decisions for the corporation. It felt real good to know that we had brothers in key management positions at Digital because they did not exist at RCA, Sperry, CDC or Philco Ford when I was there. But after meeting each of these executives, I was embarrassed and disappointed. They had all of the trappings and perks of an executive but they had not earned the real respect of their peers.

Let me explain to you what I mean. Let's start with *John Strawboss* who was on the staff of Ken Olsen, the President. Well, to some of the Black employees *John* could do no wrong but to many others *John* was a joke. I remember the first time I saw him in person at the National Urban League Conference in Washington, DC. Digital was a major supporter of the Urban League especially with the Job Opportunity Showcase. For this event, Digital provided computers and personnel to assist in helping people attending the convention to do a job search on a computerized database. Prior to the opening of the event, Digital would usually have a meeting of all of its employees who were supporting the conference. The majority of the people supporting this conference were Black and *John* took this opportunity to address the employees.

John was a very pompous individual. You almost felt like he wanted you to give homage to him as though he was the Pope. He was a real HNIC and he wanted everyone to know it. He talked down to the people as though we were a bunch of kids. I learned later that *John* was twelve days older than I was and that certainly did not qualify him as being old enough to be my father. I must admit that I had a personal experience with *John* that rubbed me the wrong way and it probably biased my opinion of him. I understand that he did some wonderful things in the Boston area but my comments are based on what I saw and heard.

What happened was I sent a copy of some material for a self-esteem program for young people for *John* to review. My purpose for sending this information to him was that I wanted Digital to consider sponsoring this program for schools as part of a community service program. All such programs had to be approved by *John's* department. I was not upset with *John* because he did not approve it but I did not like the way he did it. After several unsuccessful attempts to reach him, I finally told his secretary that I needed a yes or no answer because I wanted to give Digital the first right of refusal. So when she told him this, he finally came to the phone and said this to me, *"I'm evil as hell today because I have a cold and I don't care what you do with your program because we're not interested!"* End of conversation. Now I must tell you that *John* did not know who I was except that I was a Digital employee. This was not the way for a senior executive or anyone to talk to an employee.

The next time I saw *John* was at another Urban League convention. But this time, I was walking around the exhibit area with my sister-in-law Caroline Jones. Well *John* was quite fond of her but he did not know who I was. After she introduced me to him, she said to him, "have you heard Aubrey's self-esteem tapes because they are quite good." He said he remembered receiving them, but he had been too busy to listen to them. He suggested that I take the tapes to some lady in the Digital booth and tell her that he said she should listen to the tapes. Caroline already knew the story but perhaps *John* was just trying to cover himself and make a good impression on Caroline. Needless to say, I did not follow up with *John* anymore.

The final thing on *John* was his farewell speech to the Black employees at yet another Urban League convention. He told us that he was not being forced out but that he had a great opportunity to work on some ventures in South Africa. He said that before he leaves the company he was going to have "A real come to Jesus meeting with the new president of Digital." I don't know how many people believed him but I did not. There was a strong rumor that after the founder, Ken Olsen, was forced to retire that *John* would not be far behind. *John* did leave and I wish him well.

The other HNIC was quite a different person. In fact, he was a folksy down-home guy not very presumptions in his demeanor. He was a regional vice president for sales at the time. Most people had nice things to say about *Al Goodfeller*. An easy going person who did not like to make a lot of waves and perhaps because he was able to go with the flow, he survived. I was very disappointed when I first saw *Al*. We were at an all Digital function and he sat at a table next to me and acted as though I was not even there. It is true he did not know me but I had on my Digital badge and I had hoped that he would have at least spoken to me. I finally got a chance to meet him when he visited our office. He was very cordial to me. But the thing that bothered me was what the Whites would say about him behind his back. Undoubtedly, a lot of it was envy but some of the things were apparently true.

Basically, they complained about some of his Black staff. In fact, one of the sales DMs confided in me that he had a real problem with some people on Al's staff but did not know how to handle it. This sales DM at the time was my boss and expected me to have some special insight because all of the people he was talking about were Black. He just came right out and said that he did not feel that two of *Al's* staffers were competent and that *Al* needed to do something about it. His problem was that *Al* was his boss and he did not know how to tell him. My suggestion to him was to bring it to *Al's* attention and then discuss his specific concerns with *Al.*

The difference between *Al Goodfeller* and *John Strawboss* was that I had empathy for *Al* because he was in tough position with everybody trying to second-guess him. I will confess, that even I was guilty of that too at times. But I felt sorry for *John* because he obviously needed to put up the big front to make himself feel important. He needed the brothers and sisters to sing "Hail to the HNIC."

Valuing Diversity

There was a lot of talk about valuing diversity in the corporate world and especially at Digital. We were supposed to be a model company of how to successfully implement a valuing diversity operation. I attended a number of seminars conducted by Human Resource consultants. I must admit that Digital probably did a better job in this area than most corporations. A young man in the Blue Bell office had AIDS and the company was very supportive of him. Human Resources had employee meetings to discuss any concerns people might have working with a victim of AIDS. The victim himself spoke to the group and answered most of the questions that were on people's minds. He made the point to everyone that he was "living with AIDS and not dying with AIDS." A magazine did a story on the employee and his manager and how each dealt with the news and the impact on each of them. Digital gets an A+ from me on how they handled AIDS in the workplace.

Probably one of the most interesting things that happened at Blue Bell was that an employee underwent a sex change. The "he" became a "she." There was concern on how would employees and customers react to a person who decided to change his sex from a male to a female. I did not know the person but I did see her after the change. What they did at Digital was to prepare the employees for what to expect when an employee leaves work one day as *Bob* and returns a few weeks later as *Bonnie*. Again, Digital Human Resources department did a good job of preparing the work force. One of the interesting things that was done initially was to restrict *Bonnie's* usage of the rest room to the second floor ladies room. This was to allow the women in the office who might have felt a little bit uneasy of sharing a rest room with *Bonnie* to get used to the idea. After some period of time, the restriction would be lifted.

Another interesting incident occurred when the managers had to view a video on Valuing Diversity. In the video, there was a dramatization of how some females are treated in the workplace. More specifically, it illustrated how some female workers' suggestions and ideas are ignored by their male peers. The video illustrated the right way and the wrong way to do it. I was the only Black in attendance viewing this video together with four White females and approximately the same number of White males. When the video was over, the moderator asked for comments. One of the White managers, *Rick*, said: *"I am happy we don't have anything like that at Digital."* Now *Rick* was one of my favorite people but he was quite naive if he really believed what he said. Fortunately, another manager, *Bill*, spoke up. He challenged *Rick's* statement. So the moderator asked for comments from the females employees but none of them would say anything. When I asked one of them after the session why she did not speak up, she said that she should have but felt very uncomfortable doing so.

I learned a long time ago to stay away from three topics on the job, *racism, politics and religion* because you rarely resolve anything during a short discussion. But I could not just sit there and not say anything. So I began with a short story and it was almost like everyone was waiting for me to say something. Essentially, I told them the real problem with discrimination is that even when it's pointed out to well-meaning people they don't even recognize it sometimes. I told them the story of coming up north from the south and how some of the northern Whites wanted to know how it felt to be up north. I told them that many of the same things that were happening in the south were happening in the north. But for years, northerners would point to the southerners and say, "see we are not like them." I told them what they saw in the video still happens in Digital today. It might not be as blatant, but it happens. Everyone got real quiet and there were no more questions and the session was over. Afterwards, the moderator said to me "you were really brave in there!" I looked at her, smiled and said, "What do you mean I was brave? I just told the truth!"

Downsized Again

The economy was a lot healthier in 1987 than it was in 1994 when I was once again a casualty of corporate downsizing. In 1994, I was downsized from Digital Equipment Corporation after almost seven years. Digital was a good company with good products and good people but it made some strategic mistakes. It was a technology leader but a marketing neophyte which cost the company dearly in the end. Digital could no longer compete in the fast moving computer market, and therefore, had to reduce expenses by downsizing. As a manager, it was very difficult and stressful for me, to have to layoff so many competent people. In a sense, it seemed like downsizing was happening every quarter.

Digital Equipment Corporation like many other companies was under a lot of pressure to reduce expenses and the largest expense of a labor-intensive company is people. I remember the first downsizing at Digital because it was the first time the company ever had a layoff. The first time around was a little easier because there were people who, because of their performance, should probably have been let go. Ironically, the first group that was downsized received a very generous financial package as compared to what we received. But as the company continued to lose money the severance packages became smaller and smaller. For example, if you had twenty years of service in the first group you received nine weeks pay plus one week for every year you were with the company for a total of twenty-nine weeks pay. In addition your medical coverage was equal to the same period. When I was downsized, a person with twenty years received four weeks plus a flat eight weeks for any time of service over ten years for a total of twelve weeks pay. So the top performers who were the last to leave were rewarded less - Seventeen weeks less! Something was wrong with that picture but nobody seemed to care about it.

I was ready when it was my turn to be downsized because I was tired of telling good people that they no longer had a job. It is one of the most difficult and stressful things that you have to do as a manager. I had served my purpose at Digital and had become bored with my job long before being downsized. I hung in there because I became complacent at Digital. I had a job with a decent salary and benefits together with the freedom to pursue my writing and working with young people.

Morale was at an all time low and it was very depressing to come into the office. Everyone (who was smart) was working on his or her resume. A company that I once described as having good people and good products was losing a major resource, its people. Good technical people are a lot more difficult to replace than are non-technical people. Digital had some of the best people in its field and the competition knew it. Good technical people had less of a problem finding another job as compared to management types like myself.

Middle Management is looked upon today by many corporations as not needed. They feel that each employee should be empowered to do his or her job and that there is not any real value added by the management team. The new buzzword floating around was "Self-directed workforce" which was a code expression for getting rid of middle management. I would agree with the assessment that many of the managers add little or no value but I think some companies are being "penny wise and pound foolish" in an effort to cut expenses. They will pay an even bigger price later.

The nagging fear of being downsized can paralyze people. Consequently, morale was low and sales were down. It was a "Catch 22." One of the reasons sales remained low in Digital was because many of the employees who still had jobs assumed that they would eventually be terminated. So a majority of the people were concentrating their energy and efforts on job prospecting instead of increasing productivity to improve sales. My department went from thirty employees to six.

In 1987, when I was hired, Digital had over 125,000 employees worldwide. When I left in 1994, Digital had approximately 75,000 employees worldwide. It was rumored that the corporation's goal was to reduce personnel to 60,000 employees because that was what the new corporate financial model could support. In 1996, I learned that Digital had reduced its work force to 60,000 and that they were still planning to cut more people from the work force. Today, Digital does not exist as a separate company; Compaq acquired it and later Hewlett-Packard acquired Compaq.

Regardless of the reason for being downsized, most people experience some type of emotion. Whether you are angry, bitter or ambivalent, it's okay to have these feelings. To be in touch with your feelings is human and normal after a downsizing. Acknowledge your feelings; but if you get down; don't stay down. Vent your feelings, accept what happened to you as just another challenge in your life and then move on. That's exactly what I did the last time I was downsized. Not only was I able to deal with my downsizing, but I also helped a number of people to get on with their lives. A lot of time, in my last days at Digital, was spent counseling employees, including some managers, on what they should do next. I helped many people with their resume and marketing strategy for selling themselves. It was really sad to see a once thriving company like Digital to hit the skids. Top management at Digital has to shoulder a lot of the blame for a lack of a real vision and a realistic strategy for the economic times of the day.

Being downsized from Digital help set me free. Although I knew it was time for me to leave, I was still somewhat reluctant to go out on my own. I had this New Emancipation Proclamation but I still was not sure that I was ready for my freedom. I, like the freed slaves, was still looking for the security of the plantation. I used to go to Drake Beam and Morin Outplacement Service and would search their job lead database. This was a computerized database that allowed you to search for jobs based on the criteria that you entered. During my search, I was still looking for corporate management jobs in planning, marketing and general management. I networked with a number of people trying to find leads to opportunities. All I was looking for was an opportunity to work in an environment where I could add value and be appreciated. But what I learned was that some people might want to help, but they don't know how to help you. Some will give you lip service while others won't do anything, including returning your phone calls.

I knew I had all of the skills to start my own management consultant business, but I kept telling myself, *"I did not want to start my own business at this stage of my life!"* I believed in the 20-20-20 theory. The first 20 years of your life you spend getting an education. The next 20 years you spend gaining experience and on-the job training and the third 20 years you get ROI (Return on Investment). What I failed to realize was that the ROI could be achieved by working for myself. Sometimes old habits are hard to break. Although we know better, sometimes we continue doing those same things because it is comfortable and we don't like change. To make a change meant leaving the security of the plantation and like most slaves I was afraid to leave.

The thought of starting my own business did not interest me for a number of reasons. I knew that being a successful entrepreneur would require a real commitment. A person works harder for himself than for someone else. I rationalized that at this stage in my life, I wanted to take it easy for a while. I had become very complacent in the corporate environment. I had a comfort zone and thought that I would stay until retirement which was five years away. But reality set in. I was downsized and I knew that I did not want to work for another large corporation. I had done that and had been there too many times. It was time for a change. So I looked at my options. I realized that I was not ready to retire, I had skills and experiences that the market was buying, so why not try doing my own thing? That's what I finally did.

After 25 years in management working for five Fortune 100 corporations, I decided not to work for anyone anymore. I formed Aubrey Jones Associates, A Planning, Marketing and Management Consultant firm. This business helped give me the freedom to leave the plantation and also allowed me to do some other things I enjoyed doing. In addition to the Consulting business, I started writing some motivational poems and books for young people which I published myself. Later, I formed a new company called **"I Can Do It Too!" Inc.** My company expanded to include consulting, training, publishing and workforce development. We specialized in entrepreneurial, motivational and instructional programs for all ages. What I did was to form a company that included those things I do best and enjoy most. The good news was that I was now free to pursue anything that I wanted to do. *I was no longer on the plantation!* I finally learned, after many years on the plantation, *that there was life after RCA and even a much better life after Digital.*

X. How to Get off the Plantation

This entire chapter is guide to what it takes to get off and stay off the invisible plantation. It includes some additional lessons I learned from the "school of hard knocks," which helped me overcome the obstacles I faced. It is intended to be motivational with messages for people of all ages.

Are You Ready to Leave the Plantation?

"If I could have convinced more slaves that they were slaves, I could have freed thousands more."
Harriet Tubman

After the Emancipation Proclamation was issued, many slaves did not want to leave the plantation. They had nowhere to go because they knew nothing except life on the plantation. They were afraid to face the world. I can imagine some of the slaves saying, *"I'm going to stay on the plantation as long as they feed me, house me and don't whip me because life is pretty good."* Some slaves would rather stay there than be free. Some of the corporate slaves (including myself) also became too complacent and enjoyed, what we thought, was the security of a having a job for as long as we wanted to work. Whether or not we wanted to be free, downsizing removed our sense of security and set some of us corporate slaves free.

Today, many college graduates are still living at home. They do not have the urgency or desire to make a change. Many of us, as parents, have made it too easy for our kids and they have become too complacent. I am happy to be able to help my daughter but she needs to accept the challenges in her life if she wants to accomplish anything. Many of the young people today want the big cars and the fine clothes. They want it now but they are not willing to pay the dues necessary to get these things. No one is saying it's going to be easy. But the young people have to learn how to deal with the hand they have been dealt. Some blame others for their problems. Rather than look for ways of how to succeed, they make excuses which are really reasons to fail. Many young people are still living on their home plantation and don't want to leave it.

In my kitchen, there is a quotation on my bulletin board. I don't know who to give the credit to for this wonderful quote but I use it often. This quote is, *"We are faced with a series of great opportunities brilliantly disguised as impossible situations."* I learned that the system could control where I lived, where I went to school, where I sat on the bus, and where I drank my water but it could ***not control*** how I think unless I allowed it to do so. I alone have the freedom to dream my dreams, set my goals and make it happen. **The invisible plantation was created by me.**

It was all mental and **all I needed to do was to stand up and step off the plantation** because there was nothing keeping me there but myself. As a Christian, I believe that *"I can do all things through Christ who strengthens me!"* **You see, I realized that God has my back.** But I had to take the first step and once I took that step coupled with my belief and desire, the next steps were revealed to me. I certainly am not minimizing the problems and hardships in this world, but neither will I allow them to control my life again. I will not allow a negative attitude to control my mind to the point that it consumes me. *I left the plantation and I shall not return!*

My Attitude–Controls My Altitude

By Aubrey B. Jones, Jr.

> Life is 10% of what happens to me
> And 90% of what my reaction will be
> My attitude controls my altitude
> My attitude controls my altitude

How I think, determines the way that I act
How I act, determines the way that others react
If I think I am inferior, then I will act inferior
If I act inferior, others will think I'm inferior too
If I think I am important, then I will act important
If I act important, others will think I'm important too
My attitude counts in everything that I do
At home, at school and especially on the job too
My attitude reflects my actions and what people see in me
I am what I think I am, and that's what people see

> Life is 10% of what happens to me
> And 90% of what my reaction will be
> My attitude controls my altitude
> My attitude controls my altitude

Stuff happens in this world today
So I've learn to deal with it in a positive way
I turn a negative situation into a positive one
And that is easier said than done
A positive attitude is really good
But that's hard to find in my neighborhood
Thinking positive might seem outrageous
But a positive outlook is really contagious
I have a positive attitude you see
Because my attitude determines how successful I'll be

> Life is 10% of what happens to me
> And 90% of what my reaction will be
> My attitude controls my altitude
> My attitude controls my altitude

There's Life After Downsizing

Downsizing impacts the way people look at the corporate plantations today. Success today probably has a different meaning than it did before downsizing. For example, if you were a workaholic and never took any time out for yourself or your family, it really did not matter to the company when it decided to downsize. Your good job performance might have delayed your downsizing for a while but eventually it caught up with you. From a company's perspective, your downsizing was purely a business decision.

The future plantation workers won't put up with what we put up with in the past. There are no more contracts. Every person is for himself or herself. There is no more loyalty on either side. Many of the young brothers and sisters are not willing to put up with the stuff that their forefathers had to put of with. Even worse, some of the young brothers and sisters don't know or even want to know about the past. Today, many of the young brothers and sisters are smarter and much more affluent then we were. But they live in the microwave society where they expect things to happen instantly. They want instant success. They don't want to wait. And unfortunately, many of them don't even want to work for it.

Maybe you might not want to leave the plantation even after downsizing. So you search for a new job and find a position on another plantation. Probably, like most people who start a new position, you will be excited and raring to go. You will want to perform well on the job and hope that you won't have to look for a job again. But there is no such thing as job security anymore. Regardless of your attitude or performance on the job, downsizing could happen again. There are a number of factors beyond your control such as potential re-organizations or cutbacks resulting from a merger or acquisition. A few years ago, employees at IBM and Digital Equipment Corporation probably thought that they had a job for life or at least until they retired. They probably felt that if they worked very hard and did everything the employer asked them to do; they would have a contract for life. But the contracts were broken. Today, there are no guarantees and you have to plan to live by the new rules on the corporate plantation.

The new rules suggest that you be prepared! Economic uncertainty can cause factors beyond your control and you should not allow yourself to be caught unprepared. Stay on top of your market value and your career by constantly educating yourself. Develop a plan for your personal and professional development. If you are not doing so already, save some of your salary for the next rainy day. After going through a downsizing, you learn a lot about yourself that will help you in your next position. You probably spent considerable amount of time studying, analyzing and marketing yourself. Don't let it go to waste. Use this new found knowledge to help you move ahead. You made some new contacts through networking, so don't forget to call or write them to let them know about your change of status. Thank them for their help and stay in touch because you never know when you might need them again. Remember that you learn what you live, and that there are a lot more important things in life than having a job.

Finally, many companies are focused on the bottom line, which means fewer employees, benefits and perks. Benefits and rewards that you were accustomed to receiving in the past are either cut back or gone. Corporations are running "leaner and meaner" these days. With the new technological breakthroughs (Cell phones, Palm Pilots, the Internet, etc.), company expectations for employee productivity are up. So how should this affect you on your next job? Or simply, "what should this mean to you?" It means that you should *"get a life"* if you don't have one already. Don't let your job put too much stress in your life because life is more than just getting up and going to work every day. You must place a higher value on relationships with your family and friends. Take time out for yourself. So before you accept a new job, make certain that you understand what is expected of you and know how you will accomplish it. ***Don't just make a living but get a life because*** "there is life after downsizing!"

Don't Let Your Pride Get In the Way!

"God sets himself against the **proud** but he shows favor to the **humble**." (James 4:6)

Humility is not low self-esteem but godly high esteem

Pride leads to disgrace, but with humility comes wisdom. (Proverbs. 11:2)

Pride leads to arguments; those who take advice are wise (Proverbs 13:10)

Proud people seldom realize that **pride** is the problem, although everyone around them is aware of it.

Pride is something that you must swallow too if all that it's doing is hindering you.

Stay in School

The slave masters were able to control their slaves by keeping them in the dark and denying them information. They would not let the slaves learn how to read or write. Today, the slave masters don't have to keep our young people in the dark. Some of our young people are keeping themselves in the dark. What is even more disturbing to me is that some of the students don't even care about school. They are not motivated to learn and are just wasting their time in school.

For example, I spoke at a Middle School in Philadelphia and some students did not like what I had to say. It was Black History month and I was trying to tell the students about some of our Black heroes. One of the students asked, *"Why you talking about that stuff; we've already heard about that enough."* His remarks shocked, hurt and angered me. I did not say much more that day because I did not know what to say. He completely caught me off guard. So when I went home, I thought about what he said, and then decided to write a poem. The next day, I called the teacher and asked if I could speak to the class again. When I returned to the school and recited my poem, the young man said that he did not mean to say all those things and he apologized. The poem was entitled, *"I'm Cool, I'm Bad and I'm Almost Grown"* and is included in this section. I turned a negative situation into a positive one because this poem is very popular among the students today. It has upbeat music recorded in rap-like style with a clear positive message about Black History.

But the question is, "how are students ever going to get off of the plantation with no skills and no respect for their heritage?" There is a lot of lip service about improving education in America. But the fact is that many of our students are failing to achieve the basic educational requirements. So what do we do about this major challenge? If our young brothers and sisters can't master the 3R's and can't use computers, they will be trapped on the plantation for the rest of their lives.

We can't afford to give up on our young people. They need us and we need to change our thinking and the way that we do things. We need to prepare our young brothers and sisters to leave the plantation. We can't just tell the young people how to do it; we need to show them. We need to help them build their self-esteem and help them feel good about themselves. Because when you feel good about yourself and believe that you can do something, then you have taken the first step to making it happen for you. If we can help build the moral and spiritual values of young people, then they will be better prepared to survive away from the plantation.

Building self-esteem alone is not the total solution to helping students achieve. We must challenge them and make them think. I told several of my friends that Black men cannot afford to retire because we have to recycle ourselves and become role models for the young brothers and sisters who do not have one. We need to "pull the coattails" of young people and mentor them on survival skills for today. We need to teach them how to take things that are working against them and make those things work for them. We need to show them how to turn negatives into positives and weaknesses into strengths. But more importantly, we must provide them the resources and support system needed to make a successful transition from the plantation.

In 1991, some Black students walked out of Overbrook High School in Philadelphia, Pa. because they said that the teacher was a racist. This incident received a lot of news coverage in the city. But one thing troubled me the most. An editorial in the *Philadelphia Inquirer* reported that Black kids don't like to study because they feel that's ***acting White!*** I was so upset after reading the editorial that I wrote a poem hoping that one day I could share it with my young brothers and sisters. I envisioned myself on the stage at Overbrook High School's auditorium sharing a message on why they need to stay in school. We have to let Black students know that too many people have made sacrifices so that they can do the things they are able to do today. It would be a shame for them to let all that effort go to waste. We need to tell them that it's time to leave the plantation. But before they can leave the plantation they need to stay in school, do their best, and graduate.

I have recited the poem, *"Message to My Brothers and Sisters,"* at a number of schools but not at Overbrook (Poem is included in this section). Each time I recited this poem, I received a positive response from my audience. The students heard me but I don't know if I really changed any minds. This poem is also included on an audio tape and is a part of the "I Can Do It Too!" program developed for schools. If I made one student think about staying in school and not giving up because of a few challenges, then the poem has met my objective. Young people will never have the chance to survive in the 21st century if they don't finish school. Too many young people are taking school lightly. They look for any excuse not to go to school and as a Black man who grew up under segregation and survived life on the plantation, it is painful for me to watch kids throw away opportunities.

Stay in school and do your best!
You can't have it now unless you work for it first
"Please don't blow any opportunities given to you!"

I'm Cool, I'm Bad and I'm Almost Grown
By Aubrey B. Jones Jr.

I'm Cool, I'm Bad and I'm Almost Grown
I Can Do It All on My own

I spoke at a school the other day
And some students did not like what I had to say
One young man asked me why was I making so much fuss
About people who were beaten, jailed and died for us
Then he said very defiantly
"I didn't ask those people to die for me"
"So why do you keep talking about all that stuff
I've already heard about that enough!"
Then, he put his head on his desk and began to mumble
"I don't care about Rosa Parks" he grumbled
"All that stuff is history
And it doesn't have anything to do with me"

I'm Cool, I'm Bad and I'm Almost Grown
I Can Do It All on My own

I was shocked, hurt, angered - All rolled into one
Because of what this *misguided* young man had done
His attitude spoke louder then the words that he had said
Because he represents a lot of students who have been mislead
His attitude said that I can do it on my own
Because ***I'm Cool, I'm Bad and I'm almost Grown***
And you can't tell me anything, you see
Because ***I already know*** what is best for me

I'm Cool, I'm Bad and I'm Almost Grown
I Can Do It All on My own

I couldn't say much more to the class that day
Because I really didn't know what more I could say
They really caught me off guard
Because I didn't expect them to be so hard

But now that I have had time to reflect
I am going to tell them something about **Respect**

> *If you're cool and bad and almost grown*
> *Here is something that you should have known*

Respect is something that you must earn
And it is also something that you can learn
Respect yourself is the first thing that you should do
And then others might respect you too
Respect your parents, teachers and all people of authority
To survive in this world and live in this society
Respect the fact that your roots are in Africa
And that your ancestors overcame a lot of things in America

> *If you're cool and bad and almost grown*
> *Here is something else you should have known*

You didn't have to ask your ancestors to make a sacrifice for you
It was something that they wanted to do
Things are much better for you today
But just remember that it was not *always* this way
You were *not* born a slave today
Because Harriet Tubman and others escaped on the Underground Railway
You don't have to move to the back of the bus
Because Rosa Parks and others boycotted for us
You have more civil rights today
Because Martin Luther King showed us a non-violent way

> *If you're cool and bad and almost grown*
> *These are some that things you should have known*

I know I can't tell you anything today
Because you already know what is best for you, so you say
I know I can't tell you what to do
But please don't *"diss"* those people who *paved the way* for you
When you *can admit* that you didn't make it this far on your own

Then you're really cool, you're really bad and you've really grown.

Message to My Young Brothers and Sisters

By Aubrey B. Jones, Jr.

Racism is alive and well today
Although some people might dispute what I say.
Let me tell you what is disturbing to me
Is to hear young people *use racism to cop a plea.*
I read in the newspaper the other night
That some African-American students equate
success in school with *"acting-white."*
What is *"acting-white"* you might ask?
Is this an excuse for not completing a task?

Is *"acting-white"* learning to read and write
working hard, getting good grades and
"doing what's right?"

"Doing what's right?"

*"What are you talking about old man?
You're out of touch and you don't understand."*

Yes I'm old enough to remember segregation.
And I remember how we fought for integration.
I'm old enough to have ridden on the back of the bus.
And I remember those freedom fighters who died for us.
I remember how the schools were under segregation.
And how we *longed* for equality in education.
So perhaps you can understand why I'm not happy to hear
About a growing lack of interest in attending school each year

I wonder what Martin Luther King would say
If he knew what some of the students are doing today.
I wonder what your forefathers would do sometimes
If they knew that you're in school just wasting your time.
Now I'm not insensitive to your plight
But what you need to do is to do what's right.
When I was in school I wasn't the smartest
But when it came to effort I worked the hardest.

*"There you go again old man,
Talking like an out-of-touch African-American!"*

Okay young people just hear me out
Although you still might have some doubt.
Doing what's right from my point of view
Is doing the things that bring the best out of you
Doing what's right when dealing with a bad situation
Is rising above it and getting a good education.

The world is neither all black or all white
And we're all created equal by a constitutional right.
So you have to learn to live with people of different races
If you expect to survive in this world and to go places.
I understand what you might be going through
Because I've had some struggles and challenges too.

But the secret to my success to date
Is that I *refuse* to let anyone else determine my fate.
Now here's the last thing I want to say
I hope you understand where I'm coming from today
I *know* you can do what you want to do
But please don't blow any opportunities given to you.

If You Get Down Don't Stay Down!

Despite how positive you try to be, occasionally something happens in your life that brings you down. When I am down, I try not to stay down too long. One time I was really feeling down over something that happened at work. When I got home, there was a book on the table entitled *"How to get up when you are down."* I don't remember the name of the author but I know my wife left it out for me to read. It was a short book and the one thing that I remembered from the book was this. *"When you have done everything you can possibly do and you still see no changes then it's time for you to take your eyes off of yourself and put them on someone else."* I really understood that message because essentially it was what I have tried to do all my life but I just never articulated it quite that way.

Probably the lowest point of my life to date was the illness and death of my first wife in 1985. Shortly thereafter, my computer books which had been doing extremely well stopped selling and then I got downsized from RCA. When things start to go wrong they go wrong. Fortunately for me, I had a support system; otherwise I could not have made it. I grew up with the notion that men are supposed to be tough and that you should never cry. As a young man, I had always heard people say, "Big boys don't cry," "Don't be a sissy," "Be strong!" and "Hang tough!" This macho attitude was instilled in us as boys and it still remains with many of us today as men.

There is a new attitude today, however. More people realize that men are entitled to express their emotions any way they would like, including crying. We see football players, basketball players and many other sports heroes cry. We saw our men in the Persian Gulf war cry. So if anyone tells you that you are not supposed to cry, then he or she has the problem and not you. I shed many tears when my wife was ill and died of cancer. I was not ashamed to cry because I felt better after I cried. I realized that crying did not make me weaker but it actually made me stronger.

The following poems, "I'm A Man but It's Okay to Cry!" and "You're Not a Bum to Me!" were written with empathy for the brothers who live in poverty with no education and no jobs. "I'm a Man but it's Okay to Cry" attempts to give a simple message to men of all ages. That is, you don't have to be ashamed to cry. The second poem was based on my encounter with a homeless man on the streets of Philadelphia. He was surprised that I took the time to talk to him. I offered to buy him some food but he said that he was not hungry. Further, he confessed that if I gave him some money he would just buy some drugs. I felt helpless because I did not know what I could do for him. So I just listened to him and prayed for him. Some brothers have a reason to cry. But after the crying, they need to gather themselves because there is still hope. They live in America and not a third world country. A plantation in this country, as imperfect as the system might be, is far better than working on plantations in many other countries. Working on a plantation in America does not have to be a lifetime sentence. You can escape! But you have to want to escape and remember that *if you get down, don't stay down.*

I'm A Man but It's Okay To Cry
By Aubrey B. Jones, Jr.

Say my brother, what's happening in this world today?
Everybody is talking about us but nobody has anything good
 to say.
Why is everybody bashing us?
Don't they have anything better to discuss?
The sisters say that we're no good
And that we're a disgrace to the neighborhood.

It's hard for me to face life
When I can't support my children and my wife.
I know that I should try to be a role model for my son
But I can't let him see me crack under the gun.
I know that a man is supposed to be strong
But I just can't put up with this pressure for long.

> *I cry sometimes, I really do*
> *And I'm not ashamed to tell you*
> *I'm a man - but it's okay to cry*
> *I'm a man - but it's okay to cry*

Everybody tells me that I should find a job somewhere
But there aren't any jobs for anyone, anywhere.
I'm too proud to let anyone know how I feel
But I am too smart to be talked into a drug deal.
Sometimes I just want to hug my wife and kids
And ask them not to give up on me while I'm on the skids.

Sometimes I just want to yell out "I need help y'all"
But I'm too proud to ask for any help at all.
I really need help but what can I do?
Is there someone around who can see me through?
Maybe I'll ask God in a prayerful voice?
I can't go wrong if I make that choice.

> *I cry sometimes, I really do*
> *And I'm not ashamed to tell you*
> *I'm a man - but it's okay to cry*
> *I'm a man - but it's okay to cry*

Men don't cry we've always heard
But now we realize that's absurd.
Men have always cried
Although it was something we tried to hide.
Men felt that crying was wrong
For any man who was suppose to be strong.

Crying is okay for men to do
Because it releases the pressure inside of you.
We see more men crying today
Because they realize now that crying is okay.
All types of men cry — they really do
And I realize now that crying is okay for me to do too!

You're Not A Bum to Me!
By Aubrey B. Jones, Jr.

> A man is whatever he thinks himself to be
> And you **need** to see what I see
> **A man who is not a bum to me!**

I was walking down the street the other day
When a man passed me going the other way
He looked at me and said, *"I'm a Bum,"* and nobody cares about me
I'm a Bum! Look at me! I have no job, I have no teeth, and I'm carefree!
I'm a Bum! If you gave me money, I'd go buy some drugs because I'm an addict, you see
I don't rob anyone or steal from anyone because there is still some honesty left in me
"I'm a Bum! I'm a Bum! Just look at me, man! What am I going to do?"
He was yelling out for help and needed someone to talk to
So I stopped, looked into his eyes and said to him, *"I don't see a bum!"*
He looked surprised, so I said it again, *"I don't see a bum!"*

> A man is whatever he thinks himself to be
> And you **need** to see what I see
> **A man who is not a bum to me!**

I'm looking at you and you're not a bum to me
I'm looking at you and let me tell you what I see
I see a man who is down on his luck and doesn't know what to do
A man who is lost in a community that no longer cares about
    you
I see a man who needs to take ownership of his situation
A man who needs to be responsible for his destination
I see a man who must call on God to let the healing begin
A man whose healing that must start from within
I see a man who can be whatever he wants to be
But he must say to himself *"It's up to me!"*

    A man is whatever he thinks himself to be
    And you **need** to see what I see
    A man who is not a bum to me!

    God Bless You Man!
    God Bless You!

Family Values

During slavery, slaves had no real control or say over their children. Their children could be abused, taken away or even killed by the slave masters. Even today some children are still abused, kicked out of the house or even killed in their neighborhoods. It is a real challenge to raise kids today especially in the Black community. **Black-on-Black Violence** is spreading like wildfire throughout our society causing African-American families serious stress and much anxiety. Walking in some neighborhoods is not safe in any state because gunfire is constant and murder is rising at an alarming rate. There used to be a time when brothers and sisters would speak to each other whether they knew you or not. But now we are afraid to speak to anyone or even look at someone the wrong way without the fear of being shot. (I wrote a poem entitled ***Black on Black Violence*** which addresses this problem and is included in this section of the book.).

Why do we have so much violence today? Is it because of a decrease in family values, and a lack of respect for authority by young people in their homes? There are many reports, studies and discussions on family values and how these values have deteriorated over the years. One major change that impacts family values is the increase in the number of single family homes. More single parents are raising kids and this impacts the family life. We sometimes feel guilty as single parents, and therefore, we often try to make up for the missing spouse by being more permissive with our children. Some families, where both parents live at home, have similar problems due to work schedules or due to a philosophy which does not encourage disciplining their children. But children need to learn how to obey authority at home. Parents need to just say "no" to their children, so that they will know who's in charge. When children learn to obey authority at home they will be better prepared to deal with authority outside of the home.

I have a friend who was a single parent and she was having the typical problems many parents are facing today raising their children. She inspired me to write the poem "Family Matters."(Included in this section). In this poem, I have attempted to address the challenges of disciplining kids that she and other single parents face. I have also included a poem called "Kids Rights" which is a parent's satirical response to those kids who try to lay a guilt trip on them about their rights. Most parents can relate to this poem and appreciate it.

Parents need to let their children know that they are "in charge." And as long as the children stay in their house, they must obey the rules. The Bible provides clear instructions for the relationship between children and parents. Ephesians 6:1-3 reads: "Children, obey your parents in the Lord: for this is right." "Honor your father and mother!" This is the first of the Ten Commandments that ends with a promise. And the promise is: If you honor your father and mother, you will have a long life, full of blessing.

Now there is a difference between obeying and honoring. To obey means to do as one is told; to honor means to respect and love. Adult children are not asked to obey domineering parents. However, young children are to obey their parents while under their care, **but they are to honor their parents for life.** When children obey their parents, they will learn that "No" means "No." Children who obey their parents learn the "good side of No." That is, they will learn later in life that obeying their parent's authority as a child "is for their own good." When my kids used to complain about how tough I was on them, I would tell them that I was not half as tough as the world was going to be on them. Now that they are older and successful, they appreciated my tough love and have learned the good side of being told "No."

When I was growing up, Blacks had a common goal, a common cause and a common need that held us together. We wanted to be able to get a good education and earn enough money to raise our standard of living. My wife and I struggled to send our kids to private school in Philadelphia so that they would have a good basic education. We also paid our kids tuition for college so that they would have some advantages that we never had. We wanted to give our kids an edge over others who did not have the same level of support that they had. But that edge meant nothing if our kids did not take advantage of the opportunity. I used to tell my kids that having the edge is like running a race. If you are racing someone who can run as fast as you and if you get a head start; then the only way that he or she will catch you is if you slow down. So I told them to keep on running!

Some parents worked two and three jobs to put their children through college. They wanted to make life easier for their kids. They did not want their kids to suffer what they had to go through. But in doing so they created a big dilemma for themselves. How do they make it easier for their children, and at the same time help them to develop a desire to succeed? Additionally, how do parents teach their children to maintain the work ethics and the moral standards of their generation? I realize that things are tough today for young people growing up in America. I know that they have to deal with drugs, violence and the threat of AIDS, something unheard of when I was growing up. It is feared by many that this is the first generation of many Blacks who will not exceed their parent's lifetime achievements.

Too many excuses are being made on why young Blacks are failing in school or can't find a job. But if the young brothers and sisters are to survive the 21st century they have to take ownership of their situation. That is, they have to recognize authority, be willing accept responsibilities, and to work hard for whatever they want to achieve. **They need to change their attitude so that they can change their world and get off the plantation they are creating for themselves.**

Children Obey Your Parents
Honor Your Father and Mother
Respect for Authority Begins at Home.
Respect for Authority Begins with "No" means "No"
Tough Love for Your Children Early Will be Good for Them Later

Family Matters
By Aubrey B. Jones, Jr.

What's going on in this world today?
There used to be a time when children
Would listened to what adults would say
But now we have this new child psychology
That encourages kids to speak out and make no apology
We used to say that children should be seen and not heard
But now we have gone from the ridiculous to the absurd
Why should we ask our children if it's okay
Instead of telling them to do what we say?
It's not cute when a little kid talks back
So why do some parents give kids so much slack?

    Children need discipline and some parents do too
    Children need discipline and some parents do too

Playing video games might seem okay to you
But games should **not** be played when there's homework to do
If you ask some parents why they're so permissive
They probably won't like it and get very defensive
It's good to give kids love and affection
But they also need moral and spiritual direction
Children need discipline and they really want it too
So why is it so hard for some parents to do?
Now here's something that I want to say
And I hope that parents will take it the right way

    Take a look at yourself and your lifestyle
    Take a look at yourself and your lifestyle

When you look at yourself what do you see?
Are you the kind of person that you'd like to be?
If you look at your parents what do you see?

Are you a reflection of how they used to be?
Now look at your children what do you see?
Are they a mirror image of how you used to be?
When your children look at you what do they see?
Are you the kind of person they'd like you to be?

If you don't like what you see after reflecting for a while
Then maybe it's time to change your lifestyle?

> Change your lifestyle before it's too late
> Change your lifestyle before it's too late

Here are a few things that some parents do
And perhaps these things might work for you too
Spend some time with your children each day
And listen with interest to what they have to say
Give them a hug and a kiss to show that you care
And do this at anytime and anywhere
Give them a little pat on the back when it makes sense
And this should give a real boost to their confidence
Now when your children don't do what you say
That's the time to start taking some privileges away

> Stand firm if you want them to respect you
> Stand firm if you want them to respect you

"Change" is difficult for most people to take
So you must stand firm on any decision you make
I know it might bother you to hear your children complain
But just say "No" because you don't need to explain
If your children don't respect your authority at an early age
They probably won't respect anyone's authority when they
become of age
Children's respect for authority is a major concern
Children's respect for authority is something they must learn

> *We learn what we live - you know that!*
> *We learn what we live - you know that!*

Kid's Rights

By Aubrey B. Jones, Jr.

Kid's have rights too.
As a parent I believe in kid's rights -I really do.

They have the right to remain silent when an adult is speaking
They have the right to do their chores without their parents
   asking

They have the right to respect their mother and their father.
They have the right to listen to their teacher.

They have the right to go to school and try to learn something.
They have the right to do their homework instead of sitting
   around doing nothing.

They have the right to ask their parents for direction.
They have the right to expect their parent's protection.

They have the right to say "No" to drug use.
They have the right to say "No" to child abuse.

They have the right to go to church and grow spiritually.
They have the right to read a book and grow intellectually.

They have the right to find a job at anytime during the year.
They have the right to start thinking about choosing a career.

They have the right to leave home if they don't like the rules.
They have the right to realize that neither they nor their parents
   are fools.

Black on Black Violence
Aubrey B. Jones Jr.

What's happening in this country today?
Brothers and sisters are killing each other every day.
Black-on-Black Violence is spreading like wildfire throughout our society
Causing African-American families serious stress and much anxiety.
Walking in some neighborhoods is not safe in any state
Because gunfire is constant and murder is rising at an alarming rate.
There used to be a time when brothers and sisters would speak to each other whether they knew you or not.
But now we are afraid to speak to anyone or even look at someone the wrong way without the fear of being shot.

We must learn to love and respect ourselves and each other.
Because if we don't love and respect ourselves, how can we expect it from another?
If you ask some people why brothers and sisters are killing one another
They will probably tell you that it is just a sign of the times and that it is going to get worse before it gets better.
They will tell you that it is because of unemployment, drug abuse, child abuse and many problems with parenthood.
They might tell you that it is because of the prevailing attitudes of *apathy*, *desperation* and *hopelessness* in the neighborhood.
But are the problems today for the brothers and sisters more challenging than what we had to go through in the past?
And are the problems today, as compared to surviving slavery and lynching, a more difficult task?
Did our forefathers dream, pray and struggle for us to kill each other?

And did Martin Luther King and others march, go to jail and die for us to destroy one another?

Some of us have become too complacent to accept the new challenges facing the Black community.
We can't depend on other people to do the job for us.
We need to accept the challenge and do it for ourselves.
We need to get back to our strengths and remember that we did it before and we can do it again.
We need to get back to our strong faith and belief in GOD and remember that all things are possible through HIM.
Parents need to go to the corners and drag their kids back home.
Politicians need to stop talking about what they are going to do and start doing something for a change.
Entertainers and Professional sports heroes need to give back to their communities if they are not doing so already.
Young people need to take a look at their priorities and realize that there are no shortcuts and that you can't have it now unless work for it first!
African-American adults need to "pull the coattails" of the young people and mentor them on survival skills for the world today.
We need to show the young people how to do it and not just tell them how they should do it. We need to lead by example!
We all must remember that life is full of obstacles and challenges and if we give up every time we are faced with a challenge we will never accomplish anything.

Stop the Violence!
Stop the Violence!

PEACE and LOVE be with you!

Lessons I Learned from My First Wife

Sometimes you get caught up in the trappings and perks of the corporate environment and lose sight of what is important in life. You become so focused and brainwashed that you forget about other things in life. As I mentioned earlier, my family was very important to me. Once I was offered a job with Xerox in Rochester, New York. After visiting the city and talking to some of the Black employees living there, I turned down the job. I told the recruiter *"Right now there is one unhappy person in my family and if I relocate to Rochester there will be four of us!"* I would not accept opportunities in a location that might be disruptive to their lives even though I might have benefited by the move. I would not take risks on ventures that would knowingly put my family in jeopardy. And I did not want my family to have to suffer because of my mistakes. So I played it safe. But I, like many other corporate slaves, put in long hours on the plantation trying to get ahead by pleasing my masters. Not only did I put in long hours but I also brought work home to do after dinner. But something happened in 1984 that gave me a totally different perspective on life. My wife became ill and she died of cancer in February 1985.

My wife was a beautiful person both inside and outside. She was a very positive person and had a strong faith in God. But it was not always like that however, because early in her life she had low self-esteem and went through periods of depression. She was always supportive of me and made me feel as though I was the strength of the family. When it came down to business and technical decisions or when a logical analysis was needed, I was the person she would come to for the answers. But I did not realize the role she played in my life until much later. As I watched her waste away in the hospital, and at home from the cancer spreading throughout her body, I could not help but to reflect back over the years on what she really meant to me. I realized that she was the real strength in our family because of her faith and belief in God. I had the physical strength, she had the spiritual strength and together we were a team each relying on the others strength.

We were married for almost 22 years and I had known her for almost 25 years, almost half of my life at the time of her death. We have two beautiful children, Aubrey III and Adrienne. I watched her grow spiritually and use her positive mental attitude to change her life and the lives of others. She went through her periods of depression for a number of years until she started listening to motivational tapes and reading motivational materials. She would try to get me to listen to the tapes and I would tell her that I didn't need to listen to those tapes because I already knew all that stuff!

Those tapes together with the Bible reading and prayer turned her life around. This shy lady with low self-esteem suddenly blossomed into this person who exuded confidence and became a person who inspired other people by her presence and her outgoing positive attitude. She would always have some positive quotes posted on the bulletin board or on the refrigerator. One of her favorite prayers was: *"Lord help me to remember that nothing is going to happen to me today that you and I together can't handle."* While she was sick, I would repeat that prayer silently each time I went to the hospital to visit her because I never knew what to expect. This prayer seemed to relax me, so I began to use it for critical situations and for major decisions at work. This was one of my secret weapons on the plantation. It was rare that I blew up on the job (although I did once or twice) because I began to realize more and more what was important. I realized that the real bottom line was *not* the plantation's profit and loss statement but your life's profit and loss statement. I realized that you can be wealthy and still be poor. You can have a beautiful house and still be homeless. You can be a slave master and still be miserable.

Life has a way of changing. Sometimes you think you have it all and in a flash it can all come tumbling down. I know because in 1983, I was making more money than I had ever made in my life. The royalties from my series of computer books were rolling in. My salary, bonuses and benefits at RCA totaled in the six figures. Then it happened. My wife died in 1985, my book sales fell due to a change in the PC market, and I lost my job at RCA in 1987.

When I lost my job in 1987, I did something that I had learned from my wife. I started to listen to some of her motivational tapes and to read some of her books. It was true that much of what I read I had heard before, but sometimes you need to revisit those positive messages. You need to hear someone else say those words so that you can internalize them. Then, you need to do what you have to do to get on with your life. I am not the same person today that I was prior to Alyce's death. I am a much stronger and better person because of what my wife taught me.

Because of my wife's influence, I write motivational materials for young people. No matter what their circumstances might be, I want the young people to learn early in life about the power of positive thinking. I witnessed what this power did for my wife. Seeing what it did for her, convinced me that it could work for others too. Today, most of the motivational materials are written for adults. I have taken the same messages for adults and packaged them in a way that it will attract young people. I use rap-like music with positive messages that have been received very well by young people and their teachers. I enjoyed challenging the system. I enjoyed doing the unexpected. I enjoyed standing up to the slave masters. But I enjoy even more working with young people and sharing with them some of the **lessons I learned from my first wife.**

Finding The Perfect Mate
by Aubrey B. Jones, Jr.

What is happening in this world today?
People get married and only half of them stay
So what about love and respect until death do us part?
It doesn't mean a thing if it is not from the heart
Everyone is looking for Mr. or Ms. Right
But don't you believe in that love at first sight
Then how do you find the mate whose right for you?
I don't have the answer but I do have a clue

> *So let's listen - for that clue*
> *So let's listen - for that clue*

Here's the first thing that you should do
Identify those things that are important to you
Then make a list of your most important points
This will be a list of your **"Musts"** and **"Wants"**
A **"Must"** is a requirement where there is no compromise
But a **"Want"** can be a concession that might be very wise
Study that list and revise it too
So it will be ready when you meet someone new

> *List your "Musts" - No Compromise*
> *List your "Musts" - No Compromise*

Suppose you see someone who looks interesting to you
Just walk up to them and say: "Hello!" "I have a survey to do"
"May I ask you a few questions? It won't take very long
"Your responses to the questions will neither be right or wrong."
So pull out your survey and read the directions
And show how easy it is to make selections
Ask for the "musts" and "wants" of all potential mates
And the responses will tell you how this person rates
Now check the list to see if it's a good match
Because this is the first step to making your big catch

> *Study your list - Is it a match?*
> *Study your list - Is it a match?*

I know that you are looking for that perfect mate
But are no perfect people in an earthly state
If you've just met someone who looks perfect to you
You're probably right if you think it's too good to be true
But if you feel that you've found the right one
Then just enjoy the relationship and have some fun
Take some time to become a good friend
Unless you decide that the relationship should end

Don't worry - There's no need to hurry
Don't worry - There's no need to hurry

But you're still undecided on what you should do
Because this person feels so right for you
"So what should I do next?", you might ask
"Make a commitment?" That's no easy task!
Now you're very excited and nervous too
Because you really don't know what you should do
Is this the right one to give my all?
Or am I setting myself up for another big fall?
Is this the perfect mate that I have been waiting to meet?
I really don't know but I'm getting cold feet

I'm really scared - What should I do?
I'm Really scared - What should I do?

Now here's something that you should know
If you're not ready for marriage then you shouldn't do so
If you truly believe that you've found the right one
What you do next depends on the Almighty One
So if you want to know if you made the right choice
Just ask God in a prayerful voice
Then leave it to Him - That's what you do
Because He is the Person to give you that clue.

Lessons I Learned from My Current Wife

After my wife died, I remained single for over thirteen years. I searched for the perfect mate. I met Diane Branch at church in 1987. We dated for almost ten years until I realized that God had provided me with the right person at the right time in my life. Sometimes we keep searching for something and learn that what we have been searching for has been right in front of us all the time. I had been searching for the perfect mate. God had already provided her to me and I was just too blind or too stubborn to realize it. I ended my search with Diane who I married in 1998. She is my perfect mate and I thank God for her.

When I was reflecting on the lessons I learned from Diane, I thought about a sermon by Pastor Alyn Waller on "Love." His message was that when you say "I Love You" that "love is a verb." We know that a verb is an action word and that "actions speak louder than words." Love acts without any guarantees and sometimes has to be tough. Diane has truly taught me that love is a verb by her actions. It's one thing to say "I love you," but it's not what you say; it's what you do that counts. She taught me that love is about giving; not getting. She is a very nurturing and giving person. She willingly gives to family, friends, others and to me. Diane is about wanting and helping others to succeed. She is like an "energizer bunny" ready and willing to help anyone at anytime. My family loves her and **so do I!** In fact, *"everybody loves Diane!"*

Diane is a very patient person and patience is not one of my virtues. I am usually on time or ahead of time for most of my appointments whereas Diane is usually a last minute person. But through it all, things have worked out well. I have helped her to schedule her time better and she has helped me to be more patient. She has a very easy going manner and always has a pleasant smile. She has helped me to tolerate people who in the past I would not have dealt with at all. When she observes me handling a situation in a negative way. She might say, "is that how a Christian should handle this?" She always reminds me that my demeanor sometimes intimidates people. Although she also knows that I'm really a teddy bear inside; and that I'm still a work in process.

Diane is my best friend. She is good for me and good to me. She keeps me grounded. She is much more trusting than I am. I remember an old saying, *"Trust not a living soul and walk carefully among the dead."* That saying somewhat describes my earlier strategy for survival on the plantation. I hope that I have changed from that person I used to be. Diane is my conscious and reminds me when I occasionally revert to my old ways. Sometimes old habits are hard to break.

Finally, she was very helpful and supportive of the "I Can Do It Too!" Program for Young People. As a principal of an elementary school, she provided insights and feedback that helped make the program a success. To get off the plantation, you have to want to get off and you need the support of your spouse to do it. I have been truly blessed because of the support and *lessons I learned from my wife.*

Thank you Diane!

I'm A Winner!

By Aubrey B. Jones Jr.

A winner never quits
And a quitter never wins

I'm a winner, you see
Because failure is not a choice for me

I look for ways to succeed
And never look for reasons to concede

I always give it my best shot
Even when others might not

I say kind words, I'm never rude
I always reflect a positive attitude

When I help someone along the way
It makes me have a much better day

Being a winner is not all about "me"
It's about helping others, that's the key

I know that I'm a winner today
Because I helped someone along the way

Don't Become Too Complacent!

A lot of things have changed since I started working in corporate America. There are a number of Blacks who crashed through the "glass ceiling" and hold prestigious, high paying positions. Today, we see Black men and women doing things that I could only dream about years ago. Sometimes, I envy them because I know I could have done the same things if I was given the opportunity. But as the Panasonic commercial used to say, "I was slightly ahead of my time." When I look back, I would like to think that I played a small role in paving the way for some of the brothers and sisters who have made it today. I want to see more and more of them to continue to do well. **But I caution them not to become too complacent because racism is alive and well today!**

Some people want to get rid of affirmative action because they say that "discrimination" is a thing of the past and that such programs are no longer needed. They argue that at universities and corporations, there is now a "level playing field." But racism is alive and well although some people might dispute what I say. Let's look at the scandal at Texaco which provides a stark picture of the *systematic* institutional racism that still exist in this country.

In 1994, Texaco—the 14th largest U.S. Corporation—was hit by a $520 million racial bias suit. The suit, filed by six African-American employees on behalf of 1,500 other employees, asserted that Texaco "systematically discriminated against minority employees in promotions and fostered a racially hostile environment."

Senior executives at Texaco allegedly were caught on tape making all kinds of racist remarks and plotting to destroy documents subpoenaed in a federal discrimination case. These tapes provided a look at what goes on every day in some corporate offices all over the United States. Dozens of Black employees testified about racist incidents at Texaco. Frequently, they were afraid to speak out at the time, for fear of losing their jobs. Allegedly, when Black employees did dare to speak out against the racism at Texaco, they were either ignored or punished.

According to news accounts, it seems that a senior executive of Texaco secretly tape-recorded meetings with other Texaco executives in which at least two damning conversations were documented on tape:

(1) The meeting participants allegedly discussed "purging the files" of incriminating racial data (a record-keeping requirement imposed by the government), evidence that had been requested during discovery by the plaintiffs' attorneys; and...

(2) The tape(s) allegedly contained racial slurs — alleged proof that Texaco execs were racists.

However, after expert audio analysis, the only "slur" that could be verified on the tape(s) was the executives' use of the phrase *"black jelly beans"* in reference to the Black employees who were suing Texaco for discrimination. (The NAACP and the plaintiffs' attorneys were later forced to admit that the N-word was not used in the recorded conversations.) On paper, Texaco was "committed to diversity" and the recruitment of "minority employees." They had "equal-opportunity programs" and glossy booklets that claimed: "Each person deserves to be treated with respect and dignity...without regard to race, religion, sex, age, national origin, disability or position in the company." But in reality, Texaco was a nightmare for Black, Latino and other oppressed nationalities.

Texaco is only one example of several major corporations that have been cited for racial discrimination. The bottom line is if you are working for a major corporation today, and like your job, and feel that you are being treated fairly, then you should stay there. But don't become too complacent because circumstances do change. And if you stay, develop a contingency plan for survival for life after you leave the plantation.

During the 1960s, we thought we had arrived because we were getting jobs in the corporate sector. I made more money in my first job than my father ever made. I had an expense account and many of the perks that went along with the position. Naively, I thought that if I worked real hard and did my very best that I could reach the top. By allowing a few of us to get the showcase jobs, the corporations could demonstrate that they were equal opportunity employers. When the government representatives did a headcount, the corporations could say, "see we have Aubrey over there and he is doing a good job." As a result, everyone relaxed a little, thinking that things were okay. The truth is that we lost a lot of the gains and momentum of the 60s because we became complacent. My message to the brothers and sisters is do not forget how far we have come. Don't forget to reach back and help someone along the way. But more importantly, don't forget to plan for the future.

The corporate plantations are getting smaller today. They are using fewer and fewer workers and the jobs are becoming more competitive. Younger workers are competing with older more experienced workers for the same jobs but for less pay. In the future, maybe careers will not be on a major plantation. Maybe you will have to start producing your own products on a small plantation, and you might have to get your hands dirty because you will not be able to hire many helpers or buy any slaves. That is, you will own your business and own the plantation. Instead of having slaves on the plantation, you will have productive and loyal partners. These partners will be respected and well compensated by the business. There are several examples where small companies gave large yearend bonuses to all employees. Not surprising, these companies are very productive, have high morale and very low employee turnover.

There are a number of very talented and capable people who are stuck on a corporate plantation. Not all corporate plantations are bad, however. Some people are well compensated for their work. But it's still a plantation. There is always the risk of downsizing if profits fall. Always save some money and live within your means. Everyone should have a contingency plan. Your contingency plan could be to do your own thing. That is, perhaps my daughter, Adrienne, who is a Fashion Designer, should think about teaming up with her peers and starting their own business. Or perhaps my son who is a software consultant should do what I was reluctant to do – start his own business. Just maybe they will defy the system and use a new model for doing business in this country. This new business model will treat people with respect and share the profits with everyone. It will help create a work environment where everyone has a personal commitment and high integrity. Is this a dream or reality? Perhaps a dream today but it could be a reality tomorrow. If the young people will use their imagination, innovation, and energy, they can change this society. **They can transform the old plantation mentality to a model organization with employees who are productive and loyal partners.**

To start your own business requires a major commitment on your part however. You have to really want it. You have to think it, believe it, eat it and sleep it. In 1998, I wrote and published a book entitled *"I'm The BO$$!"* This book introduces students to entrepreneurship. It is intended to motivate students to consider owning their own business as a possible career choice. Although written for middle and high school students, who might have an interest in becoming entrepreneurs, it is also a good beginner's book for people of all ages. I wrote this book to plant the seed, early in young people's lives, that they have choices in life. *I wanted to tell them that "you don't have to work on someone else's plantation; you can own the plantation." You Can Be The Boss!*

I'm The BO$$!

By Aubrey B. Jones, Jr.

I'm the Boss!
I take the bitter with the sweet
I take the profit or the loss
I take the ups and downs
I take the good and the bad
I work hard every day
But I wouldn't have it any other way
Because I'm the Boss!

I'm the Boss!
I make decisions and I take risks
I do the hiring and the firing
I do the planning and the marketing
I do the advertising and promotion
I do everything…
But that's okay
Because I'm the Boss!

I'm the Boss!
I keep sales up and expenses down
I keep my head up
and my feet planted firmly on the ground
I keep my customers satisfied
and my employees occupied
Being the Boss is not easy!
But that's okay
Because I'm *still* the Boss!

Success!

> *"Real success maintains personal integrity. If you are not a success by God's standards, you have not achieved true success."*
> *(Proverbs 12: 3 New Living Translation Bible Notes)*

I would like to shift gears for a moment to talk about success and some tips for getting ahead. This will be good information for everyone who wants to get off the plantation. With success comes responsibility. Some people are not successful because of "fear of failure" or even "fear of success." So how do you measure your success - By the world's standards? - Or by God's standards?

Speaking of success, I read a book entitled "What They Don't Teach You at Harvard Business School" (Notes from a Street Smart Executive). In this book, written by Mark McCormick, there was one chapter entitled **"Getting Ahead."** In this chapter, he talked about **Three Hard to Say Phrases:**
1. I Don't Know
2. I Need Help
3. I Was Wrong

I learned the power of these three phrases long before I read this book. But this book reinforces some important lessons learned.

It's amazing how many people are afraid to say **"I Don't Know."** Some people think that by using these words, they will somehow appear inadequate, dumb or even stupid. What these people fail to realize is that by not admitting what you don't know can lead to suspicion about what you do know. I remember taking a graduate course in engineering at the University of Pennsylvania. The professor was at the blackboard writing some long equations. I did not have a clue to what he was talking about. So I asked the students sitting around me if they understood what was going on. Each student said that he did not understand it either. But none of them was willing to raise his hand because they did not want anyone else to know that they did not understand. I finally raised my hand. In fact, I am never shy about asking questions if I don't understand something. I not ashamed to say *"I Don't Know!"*

"I Need Help!" People are often afraid to ask for help or accept it. Many people believe that somehow this will show that they are inadequate in their job. If they think about it for a moment, they would realize that it is a smart way for getting and receiving help. Sometimes, certain tasks are better achieved by groups than by individuals. I learned that by not asking for help is a short-sighted and narrow-minded view. But asking for help is a way to learn and a way to expand your knowledge. It is a way to expand your expertise and your value to the organization. Asking for help also demonstrates a willingness to work with others. A willingness to be a team player. I have always asked for help although I might not have received it when I asked for it. But that did not stop me for asking for help. You need to swallow your pride and ask for help when you need it. If you ask enough people, you will eventually find someone who is willing to help.

And finally, learn to say *"I Was Wrong."* Many people are afraid to make a mistake. There's a saying which you've probably heard "Show me a person who doesn't make mistakes and I'll show you a person who is not doing very much." Unfortunately, the people who are least secure about their abilities have the hardest time admitting their mistakes. To get ahead, you have to take some chances and take some risks.

Earlier in my career, I was afraid to take chances and risks because I knew that sometimes I was going to be wrong. I took the conservative approach because I did not want to lose what I had gained. I did not want to be poor again. So I took limited risks which possibly limited my advancement in the corporate plantations. But later I observed that most *successful people* took risks and usually made more right decisions than wrong ones. I also learned that successful people knew when they were wrong and were not afraid to admit it. More importantly, I learned that making a mistake - and owning up to it - are two totally separate acts. It is *not* the *mistake itself* but *how* a *mistake is handled* that forms a lasting impression. So I learned that the ability to say *"I Was Wrong"* is important because it allowed me to put my mistakes behind me. It allowed me to move on to bigger and better things and it allowed me get off the plantation.

Getting off the plantation might not be a definition of success for some people. Some people might want to stay on the plantation as long as their basic needs and some of their wants are being met. They see success in material things. I don't have anything against driving a nice car, living in a beautiful home or wearing stylish clothes. But maintaining personal integrity is more important to me. I need to look in the mirror and feel good about myself. I need to know that I have done my very best in every situation. Doing my best is providing a good product or service. If I provide a good product or service, the rewards will follow. The rewards might not be monetary but it will be the personal satisfaction that I did my best. Most of the things I mentioned above described success measured by corporate or worldly standards. Let's talk about success measured by God's standards.

Over the years, I have learned that ***real success*** is about being honest with myself and others. It's about being a blessing to someone along the way. It's about achieving goals measured by a higher standard – God's standard. Proverbs identifies two significant by-products of wise living: ***success and good reputation***. But what about people who cheated to pass a test or to get a larger tax refund – is this success? And what about the person who ignores his family commitments and mistreats his workers but gets ahead in business – is this also success? These apparent successes are only temporary. They are bought at the expense of character. Cheaters grow more and more dishonest and those who hurt others become callous and cruel. In the long run, evil behavior does not lead to success; it leads to more evil. Real success maintains personal integrity. And if you are not a success by God's standards, you have not achieved true success (Ref: Proverbs 12:3 NLT Bible Notes).

To succeed, you still have to ***believe*** that you will, because if you ***don't believe*** that you will, you probably ***won't***. If you believe you are in God's "Will," tell yourself, **"I can do it"** because God has my back. When you are in God's "Will," you will not be afraid to step out. Forget about "fear of failure" or "fear of success" - just step out on faith and just do it! Remember that **"You + God = Success!"**

But nothing comes without effort. When you are in the "Will" of God you will still be challenged. There will still be obstacles. So learn how to size up your obstacles and then determine how you are going to overcome them. Learn that prayer provides answers, and that the struggle makes you stronger. The struggle taught me how to deal with the hand that I was dealt. It taught me when to say: *"I Don't Know, I Need Help and I Was Wrong!"* Success is about being honest with yourself and others. It's about knowing "God's Will." It's about maintaining personal integrity. It's about achieving goals measured by a higher standard – **God's standard!**

Caution! Don't Let Pride Block Your Blessing.

"God sets himself against the **proud** but shows favor to the **humble**." (James 4:6)

Pride leads to arguments; those who take advice are wise (Proverbs 13:10)

"I was wrong" or "I need advice" are difficult phrases to utter because they require humility. **Pride** is an ingredient in every quarrel. It stirs up conflict and divides people. Humility by contrast heals. Guard against **pride**. If you find yourself constantly arguing, examine your life for **pride**. Be open to the advice of others, ask for help when you need it, and be willing to admit your mistakes (Notes: Proverbs13:10 NLT Bible Notes).

Pride is the inner voice that whispers, "My way is best," it is resisting God's leadership and believing that you are able to live without His help. Whenever you find yourself wanting to do it your way or looking down on other people, you are being controlled by **pride**. Only when you eliminate **pride** can God help you to become all He meant you to be (Proverbs 16:5 NLT Bible Notes).

POWER

By Aubrey B. Jones, Jr.

Life is full of obstacles and challenges.
And if you give up every time you are faced with a challenge
then you will never accomplish anything. But...

You have the *Power*
You have the *Power* in you
To do what you want to do

You need to set your goals
Dream your dreams
Don't let anyone stop you
Because you have the power

Martin Luther King used the power
to keep the dream alive
Rosa Parks used the power
to refuse to move to the back of the bus
Nelson Mandella used the power
to lead the fight against apartheid in South Africa

Everyone has the power.
I have it! You have it! Use it!

Use it—to make a difference.
Use it—to stay in school.
Use it—to accept the challenge.

You have the *Power*
Use it!—Use it Wisely!

"All Things Work Together for Good ..."

"All Things Work Together for Good to Them Who Love God, and to Them Who are the Called According to His Purpose" (Romans 8:28).

The Scriptures tell us that *"all things work together for good."* God works in everything – not just isolated incidents for our good. This does not mean that everything that happens to us is good but God is able to turn every circumstance around for our long-range good. Everything that happens to us works for good even the bad things. Sometimes things happened to me that *might not have been good* but they eventually *worked for good*. For example, I hated my first job because I had to write specifications and other documents. My plan was to design circuits and to work in a development lab. But my plan was blocked because God had a better plan for me. I did not know, at the time, that my first job would make me a better writer and would prepare me to become an author. As a result, I wrote ten books on computers.

When something happens to you, you might not always see the good in it. But oftentimes, you learn why some things happened in your life. As a Christian, you learn to be thankful. For example, "I am thankful for my family and friends because they have shown me love. But I am thankful for my detractors and enemies because they have taught me how to deal with conflict. I am thankful for my accomplishments because they have taught me how to deal with success. But I am thankful for my failures because they have taught me how to deal with obstacles." They all worked together to help shape the person that I have become today. "I'm not where I used to be nor am I where I'm going to be. I'm still a work in process because God is not finished with me yet!"

A question that I have struggled with over the years is "How can I know the 'Will' of God?" More specifically, how do I determine the overall direction of my life? Throughout this book, I have said that "I will do my best and God will take care of the rest." But how do I know when my best is God's best? The scriptures tell me that His best is His plan of action for me, not only for major decisions, but also for smaller daily decisions. That is, God's best is His "Will" for me. His "Will" is for every circumstance of my life. He might not disclose every detail about the situations I face, but He reveals specific steps I can take in order to learn and fulfill His "Will." When you are in the "Will" of God, you will not be afraid to step out on faith. If you take the first steps, God will reveal the rest. But remember that when you are in the "Will" of God, you will still be challenged. Because once you start doing God's "Will," all hell will break loose. But you need not worry or be frightened about the consequences because God is in control. You simply cannot lose when you obey the "Will" of God.

Finally, I have learned that God is not working to make me happy but to fulfill His purpose. I also have learned that His promise is not for everybody. It can be claimed only by those who love God and are called by Him. That is, those people whom the Holy Spirit convinces to receive Christ. I am one of those people who has a new perspective and a new mindset. I trust in God; not worldly treasures, because my security is in heaven; not on earth. My faith is stronger in pain and persecution because I know God is with me. As difficult as it might seem, I have learned to try to make the best out of a bad situation. I have learned that the struggle makes me stronger. And I can truly say that *"all things work together for good to them who love God, and to them who are the called according to His Purpose."*
(Ref: Rom 8:28 Notes NLT Bible Notes)

Is That You God?
Aubrey B. Jones, Jr.

How do you know when God is speaking to you?
Here are some questions to ask to see if it's true:

Is it scriptural? Is it something the Bible would tell you to do?
Is it internal? Do you feel the Holy Spirit moving inside to direct you?
Is it providential? Did someone or something unexplained occur right out of the blue?
Is there an Inner Peace? Do you feel an inner peace because God has told you what to do?

Sometimes I hear things, feel things, or see things and I wonder what this is all about
It would be so much easier to follow God's directions if He spelled everything out
God speaks to us in many ways
He spoke to Moses through a burning bush
He spoke to Paul through a bright light on the road to Damascus
He spoke to Joseph and others through a dream or vision
He spoke to Gideon through some tests to help him with a decision
But those are the ways God spoke to us yesterday
So how does God is speak to us today?
God speaks to us through the Bible, the Holy Spirit, Inner Peace and circumstances
He speaks to us through other people to reveal his plan in many instances.
But don't be fooled by *every* strong impulse or feeling telling you what to do
Because it might *not* be God speaking to you

Is it scriptural? Is it something the Bible would tell you to do?

> *Is it internal? Do you feel the Holy Spirit moving inside to direct you?*
> *Is it providential? Did someone or something unexplained occur right out of the blue?*
> *Is there an Inner Peace? Do you feel an inner peace because God has told you what to do?*

If you want to know God's plan for you today
Read the Bible to see what it has to say
You can open the Bible and meditate on a selection
Then wait on the Holy Spirit to point you in the right direction
Don't worry about anything and pray about everything
Tell God what you need and thank Him for what He's already done
If you have to make a decision, ask God to help you make the right one
Sometimes a friend who knows the Bible can help you decide on what to do
Sometimes a friend might say something, in passing, that reveals God's plan for you
God might reveal His plan for you through life's circumstances
But make sure He reveals His plan to you before you take any chances
Sometimes you know it's God's plan for you because an inner peace overcomes you
God's inner peace guards your heart against anxiety, and helps you to do what you need to do
But if you are still not sure who is speaking to you
Answer the following questions to see if they are true:

> *Is it scriptural? Is it something the Bible would tell you to do?*
> *Is it internal? Do you feel the Holy Spirit moving inside to direct you?*
> *Is it providential? Did someone or something unexplained occur right out of the blue?*
> *Is there an Inner Peace? Do you feel an inner peace because God has told you what to do?*

Epilogue
"I Can Do All Things Through Christ Who Strengthens Me!"

"Lord, I know I can't do anything without you, so I pray that your hand be with me. Lord, by your Spirit, pull off something great today for your glory."
Amen.

It is now 2005, over 10 years since I started writing this book. A number of things have happened in my life since then. ***I have left the plantation and don't plan to return.*** I have grown spiritually and have found my purpose in life. In 2000, after twenty five years, I left my previous church (Salem Baptist Church of Jenkintown) to join Enon Tabernacle Baptist Church in Philadelphia. At Enon, I received my call and my mission. I can truly say that I have grown more spiritually in the past five years than in the last forty. Sure, I went to church, taught Sunday school and volunteered for many ministries and projects at my former church. But I stopped growing spiritually. I was comfortable with going to church but I was no longer challenged to get more involved in meaningful church work. I realized that I needed more. I needed to take my life to another level spiritually.

Reverend Dr. Alyn Waller, Pastor of Enon Tabernacle Baptist Church in Philadelphia inspired me. His sermons and Bible studies helped me grow spiritually. He helped me understand why I am alive and that God has an amazing plan for me. I realized that once I knew God's purpose for me, it would give meaning to my life. For example, Pastor Waller made a comment during Bible Study that he wanted all of the young people in the church to memorize the names of all of the books of the Bible. Further, he said that he wanted the students to know at least five Bible stories. I accepted this as my assignment. As a Sunday school teacher, a Bible study leader, and a person who enjoys a challenge, I tried to come up with a simple way of helping people understand the Bible. One way to remember any new piece of information is to associate it with something you already know or to remember it in some ridiculous way. So the first thing I did was to develop a simple way to memorize the names of the books of the Bible.

To help people memorize the names of the books of the Bible, I tried using numbers. I realized that most people can remember numbers better than names. Think about it. We have to remember telephone numbers, social security numbers and PIN numbers to name a few. So when I looked at the Books of the Old Testament, I saw the numbers "5 – 12 – 5 – 5 – 12." Five (5) books of law, 12 books of history, 5 books of poetry, 5 major prophets and 12 minor prophets for a total of 39 books. This gave me the idea to draw a diagram showing the groupings of the books. This visual representation, with the numbers "5 – 12 – 5 – 5 – 12" above the appropriate box, helps to relate the numbers with the names. Finally, acronyms and rhymes were developed as memory joggers for the names of the OT books. Although some of the acronyms don't make a lot of literal sense, I did try to be logical as far as practical. For the New Testament books, a similar approach was used. The numbers, "4 – 1 – 14 – 7 – 1" represent: 4 Gospels, 1 book of history, 14 Pauline Epistles, 7 general epistles and 1 book on prophecy for a total of 27 books. Then the same procedure, used for the OT books, was followed. *It worked!* I used this approach successfully to teach students how to remember the names of the books of the Bible.

It is one thing to learn all the names of the books of the Bible but it is more important that you read the Bible. But when some people look at the size of the Bible they are intimidated because they don't know where to start. So to help people feel more comfortable reading the Bible, I developed a series of "reader friendly" diagrams, with notes, as visual guides for the reader. Each book of the Bible is summarized using a one-page diagram. Each diagram includes a summary, an outline and references to chapter and verse for that particular book of the Bible. It is possible to review the one-page summary and get a pretty good idea of what that book of the Bible is all about. The result of this effort was a manuscript for a book entitled ***Diagrams and Notes for Bible Study***. This book will **not** be a replacement for reading the Bible but is a study companion to be used with the Bible. I have used this manuscript successfully to teach several Bible Study classes. This unique book encourages more people to read the Bible because it's simple and easy to use.

When Pastor Alyn Waller gave us his vision for a new church, I realized what I had to do. I knew the real reason why I left my previous church after twenty five years to join Enon. I knew that I was called to help build the new church. I did not know exactly what my role would be but I knew that I could help. So I joined the Building Committee. At the time that I joined the Building Committee, I had a small corporation which provided self-esteem and motivational products for schools. When the church was looking for a Project Administrator, I put my business on hold and volunteered to do it for free. "It is said that if you ever find something that you will do for the good of others, and do it for free, it's probably your call."

One Sunday, Pastor Waller spoke on "How to Handle a Tough Assignment." This sermon was right on time for me. After I became the Project Administrator, I faced some immediate challenges. In his sermon, he told us that the call on your life is bigger than you can handle. That is, God wants you to depend on Him to help you. Further, he reminded us that you can't play with God's call on your life. When you receive the call, you should plan and execute with people who love God and who love and support you. When you say "yes" to God, all of His resources are available to you. Finally, act like it has already happened because with God's help you cannot fail. When you are in "His Will" God will not let your enemies win.

One of the reasons I volunteered for the Building Committee was to give something back to the Lord for all of the blessings that He has given me. I felt like I had been in training for this assignment all of my life. God had prepared me to handle any challenges that might occur on this assignment. I knew that I could handle this assignment because God had my back. All I have to do is to do my best and He will take care of the rest. The new church is scheduled to be completed by the spring of 2006. It has not been easy but I know it's going to be all right. Because I truly believe that *"I can do all things through Christ who strengthens me."*

When your situation seems impossible
Remember that God is always available
Ask God in a prayerful way
He will tell you what to do or say
Praise Him and confess your sins to Him
Thank Him and then make your requests of Him
Ask God about anything
He has the final answer to everything!

Final Quotations

"You + God = Success!"

"I have the power in me to choose what I want to be."

"All things work together for good to them who love God, and to them who are called according to His purpose." (Romans 8:28)

"Lord, help me to remember that nothing is going to happen today that you and I together can't handle."

"I Can Do All Things through Christ Who Strengthens Me!" (Philippians 4:13)

"Let your light so shine before men, that they may see your good works, and glorify Your Father which is in heaven." (Matthew 5:16)

Pride leads to arguments; those who take advice are wise (Proverbs 13:10)

"I was wrong" or "I need advice" are difficult phrases to utter because they require humility. Pride is an

ingredient in every quarrel. It stirs up conflict and divides people. Humility by contrast heals. Guard against pride. If you find yourself constantly arguing, examine your life for pride. Be open to the advice of others, ask for help when you need it, and be willihng to admit your mistakes.
(Notes:Provers 13:10 NLT Bible Notes)

"If I could have convinced more slaves that they were slaves, I could have freed thousands more."

Harriet Tubman

Printed in the United States
35554LVS00005B/133-204